THE
ENTERTAINERS

DOUG WALTERS & MARK WAUGH

THE ENTERTAINERS

TALKING CRICKET THEN AND NOW

RANDOM HOUSE AUSTRALIA

Random House Australia Pty Ltd
20 Alfred Street, Milsons Point, NSW 2061
http://www.randomhouse.com.au

Sydney New York Toronto
London Auckland Johannesburg

First published by Random House Australia 1999

National Library of Australia
Cataloguing-in-Publiction Data

Walters, Doug, 1945– .
  The entertainers: talking cricket then and now

  ISBN 0 091 84025 2

  1. Walters, Doug, 1945– —Anecdotes. 2. Waugh, Mark, 1965– —Anecdotes. 3. Cricket—
Australia—Anecdotes. 4. Cricket players—Australia—Anecdotes. I. Waugh, Mark, 1965– .
II. Title.

796.3580994

Cover photograph by Action Photographics
Cover and text design by Gayna Murphy, Greendot Design
Typeset in 11.5/15pt Sabon by Midland Typesetters, Maryborough, Victoria
Printed and bound by Griffin Press, Netley, South Australia

10 9 8 7 6 5 4 3 2 1

CONTENTS

To those supporters who enjoy cricket being
played in an aggressive way.

DOUG WALTERS

To all the fans who have supported me and
the teams I've played for over the years.
Also to my late grandfather, Edward Waugh,
who watched or listened to every game I played.

MARK WAUGH

ACKNOWLEDGEMENTS

I would like to give special thanks to my wife, Caroline, for her assistance with this book.

Doug Walters

Being involved in writing a book can be hard work, absorbing many hours. It would not have been possible to produce *The Entertainers* without the great input from Deb Callaghan. Deb has been the backbone of the book, helping to compile stories, photographs and statistics into a readable form, and I thank her for that.

To Doug, I thank you for being my co-author and for your obvious contribution to our book. And to my team-mates over the many years of my career, thank you for the greatest friendship and all the enjoyable times on and off the field.

Last, but not least, thank you to my family and in particular my fiancée, Sue Porter, for all her support and encouragement through the good and bad times.

Mark Waugh

FOREWORD

All cricketers should have a sense of humour. I would not say, hand on heart, that it is *essential* because, in the past 50 years playing in and watching the first-class game, I have come across a few who were totally devoid of that attribute. What was worse, they couldn't understand they may have been missing something in life.

Not so Doug Walters and Mark Waugh who have teamed here to bring humorous life to sixteen chapters of a book and to share a mixture of stories of then and now; I was very much in the 'then' era, as was Doug Walters, though perhaps he wasn't as *then* as I was. He and I, two Central Cumberland boys, made our first-class debuts against Queensland at the SCG. Mine was in 1948–49 and I made 2, his was in 1962–63 and he made 1. Doug was born in Dungog, NSW, and in 1961, when Jack Chegwyn took one of his touring sides there and was impressed by the 16-year-old, he asked me if I would take him under my wing at Cumberland where I was captain at the same time as I was captaining NSW. The odd thing about it is that although we played together in club cricket, and for NSW, I never once captained him in the NSW side, although we played in the same teams.

This was his fault. Not by intent, but purely the accident that had him bowling in 1963 in a club match at Mosman Oval: he found the edge and I dropped the catch at second slip and the ball, jamming my hand into the ground, broke the third finger on my right hand in three places. I missed the next Test at the MCG where Bob Simpson led Australia to victory against the South Africans, and I never captained NSW or Australia again.

Steve Waugh is the current Test captain and captured the World Cup in such brilliant style, winning seven games on the trot. In a sense he has nothing to do with this book, though he figures in it, but he was the first Waugh I knew.

When he entered Test cricket in 1985–86 he was written up as another Stan McCabe, and that is as good an example as anyone could offer concerning the damage which can be done to young players by being damned, not with faint praise, but with hyperbole. It took him several years to work out the method which suits him best and he is at the peak of his career.

Mark was the second of the family I watched. Like Norman O'Neill, with whom I played and who was a high class attacking batsman, when watching Mark I have never expected him to make me a hundred, nor would I have expected it as his captain, but whatever he makes in the future will be worth watching and paying to see. There is a touch of class about everything he does on the field, he makes it look easy when, in fact, it is all very difficult.

I know Doug Walters has a dry sense of humour, having been on the receiving end of it occasionally. By reputation Mark is the same although he's unlikely to be as dangerous as 'Bikkie' Walters who is as straight-faced a practical joker as you will find. To combine a wonderful modern-day cricketer with a star from the past, and some great stories from both of them, seems to me to be ideal.

Richie Benaud

CHAPTER ONE

HIGHS AND LOWS

I WOULDN'T
CHANGE A THING

*'I scored 155 in my first Test innings. It couldn't have
started any better if I'd written the script.'*

As anyone reflects on his or her life, it is good that the human
spirit usually helps us to recall the good times more easily than
the bad. This, coupled with the fact that I am also an optimist
who never spends any time worrying about anything, and the
fact that I tend to look for humour in serious situations, means
that I have many more highs than lows to write about.

I had a really fast rise through the lower grades of cricket. It
seemed as if I got one surprise after another. I first learned
of my selection in the NSW Colts in a phone call which came
out of the blue. Our party line, Marshdale I.U., rang with its
customary two shorts and a long. My father answered the
phone and the late Alan Barnes who was then the secretary of

the NSW Cricket Association was on the line. The all rounder Graham Southwell had withdrawn from the team that had been originally selected because of his university exams. Alan was ringing to advise me that I had been chosen to take Graham's place. I was extremely surprised because I wasn't even in the Colts' training squad at that stage. Alan assured us that it wasn't a hoax call and gave us the details of where we (or I) had to be and when.

Dad came to Sydney with me. We made the trip by train. That match was against the Queensland Colts at the old SCG Number Two Oval that has since been removed. I scored 140 not out in this, my first rep game. This is the match where the ball from one six I hit ended up in Kippax Lake across the park. Now, I know that over the years many stories grow and sixes get bigger with every year that passes, but I swear that ball did come back wet. I wasn't about to argue as to whether or not it was the same ball they fished out of the lake but I think it must have had the help of a few favourable bounces on its way there.

I followed that score with 60 against a Victorian Second XI team in the Colts' next match and then I was chosen in the NSW team to replace one of the six Test players who was not available because of Test match duties. I couldn't believe my good fortune. It was a great thrill and an honour, and I was still so young at only 16.

My biggest thrill of all time was to come a couple of years later. I had just played a game for NSW against the touring English team at the SCG. My father was visiting from Dungog and we were driving home in my Mini Minor when the news came on the radio. People talk about events which happen in their lifetime and how they remember exactly where they were and what they were doing when they heard the news. This was one such occasion for me. We were outside the Darlinghurst Post Office when they announced the first Test side to play against England in Brisbane in 1965.

The Australian Cricket Board announces its Test teams in alphabetical order so both Mark's and my names are never near the top of the list when teams are read out. I wasn't expecting to be chosen in this Test side, so when my name was tacked on the end of the list I couldn't believe my ears. I got such a shock, I had to pull my Mini over to get hold of myself. Dad and I were so overcome with emotion we could hardly talk. Many say that you have no nerves when you're young, but I can tell you, I was shaking like a leaf with excitement. This was, and still is, the thrill of my lifetime. I was ecstatic about being chosen, let alone playing. When I regained my composure, I thought of the schoolteachers I'd told about this day not too many years before.

I scored 155 in my first Test innings. It couldn't have started any better if I'd written the script. It seemed that there was to be one thrill after another, as I scored another century in my second Test in Melbourne. My bubble burst in Adelaide and my feet came back to earth pretty quickly when I got out without scoring. However, I was more than happy as I'd had a pretty successful start to my career.

That was to be as far as it went at that stage, though, because just after the completion of that series, a letter arrived in my postbox with the news that most 20-year-olds at that time were dreading. I had been called up to do National Service training and was required to report for a medical.

My medical examination didn't take very long at all because the first doctor I had to report to was an elderly man who quickly told me that he had seen every Shield game at the SCG since 1901, and added, 'You're fit enough for me'.

I managed to save enough leave to play a couple of Shield matches and two Test matches during the second year of my National Service. These Tests were against India in Australia and fortunately I played well enough to earn a tour to England in 1968 after completing National Service. I started to pick up the pieces of my cricketing career pretty well by the summer of 1968–69 when I had my best season ever. The West Indies team was touring Australia that season and I enjoyed pleasing success against them.

Along with the highs there are some lows, and I'm sure everyone has a season they would rather forget. One such season for me was 1972. It was probably the saddest time I went through. I couldn't say I was surprised when I lost my spot in the Test team for the final Test at The Oval, because, to be truthful, I thought I was lucky to have remained in the team for the previous two Test matches.

I have made light of the fact since then and often tell the story that came from that tour. My mother rang through to the dressing room at Lord's to give me some batting advice. One of the boys answered the phone and said, 'You can't speak to Doug now, he's just going in to bat'. Mum is supposed to have said, 'Then I'll wait on'. It turned out she was a very lucky woman as she got her three-minute call in anyway. Well, neither my mother nor I remember speaking that day, but maybe I would have been better off if we had because she could wield the willow pretty well.

Being dropped from a side for poor form is hard to take, but on the other hand, it makes you more determined to get back up and prove the selectors wrong. I'm not saying they were wrong in my case. The following summer in Australia, I made it back into the Test side. I wasn't an automatic selection. I had to earn the place, and luckily my form held up and I had a very good tour to the West Indies in 1973. But in the summer of 1974–75 when England toured, my position was again in doubt when I failed in the first innings of the first Test in Brisbane. Some people were calling for my head, but I was saved with a 60 in the second innings. That had done wonders for my confidence, and the team had done well, with Dennis Lillee and Jeff Thomson sending down their thunderbolts at the poor poms.

The second Test was in Perth. Greg Chappell had been dismissed in the second innings just prior to the tea adjournment, and I was next in. Ian Chappell was captain at that stage, and I knew Australia was in a pretty good position but could do with some quick runs. Ian gave me no advice, but I was most surprised when Greg spoke to me on his way out. When two batsmen cross after one is dismissed there usually aren't any words exchanged except maybe a 'bad luck', from the incoming batsman, or a 'good luck', from the outgoing team mate. However as we crossed on this occasion, Greg said, 'I got out to set it up for you so you can score a hundred in the last session'. This was unbelievable, as no batsman is ever very happy when he gets out, and Greg is no exception.

I was 3 not out at the tea adjournment, and when I came in for the break, I went up to query Greg and make sure I wasn't hearing things. He repeated the statement he'd said before as we passed. After tea I thought I might as well give it my best shot. I was batting with Ross Edwards at the time, and things began as I'd wanted. By the time drinks came on halfway through the last session, I was on 68 and thinking that if I could continue at the same rate without getting out I could be 120, or even 130, by stumps. Even though Ross Edwards was an accountant, I didn't bargain on him doing his accounting as well as he did. He scored singles off the last ball of the first three overs after drinks. Eight-ball overs were bowled at that stage, and as it turned out, Ross did the same thing to retain the strike on the last over of the day when I was on 93.

We ran through for a leg bye off the first delivery, and Bob Willis came steaming in again. His first ball to me was a bouncer which I attempted to hook, but only got the top edge of my bat to the ball and it flew over wicket-keeper Alan Knott's head and raced away to the fence. Despite the shot, it still brought four more runs and I was now on 97 with 6 balls to go.

7

With that unconvincing shot I knew I was bound to get another short ball before the over finished. The number of bouncers which could be bowled per over were not restricted then. Bob kept me waiting, and it didn't come until the very last ball of the day. Fortunately for me, bat and ball connected at the right time and over the boundary line it went. I was on 103, scoring exactly 100 in the session. I couldn't wait to hear what Greg had to say when I got inside, so off I ran.

Over the years I had pulled my fair share of tricks on many other team members, so they had chosen this time to get one back. I ran up the stairs and into the dressing room. The dressing room was empty. Everyone had gone to hide in the shower block out the back.

I decided that I was quite satisfied with the job I'd done, so I grabbed a couple of bottles from the fridge and sat down to unbuckle my pads. Ian Chappell was the first to appear. He let fly with a heap of abuse directed towards me.

'You silly so and so, why would you go and get out on the last delivery of the day? We needed you in there to score some more in the morning.' I didn't fall for that. 'Good joke', I said. 'How about taking the tops off these bottles?' Ian kept up the pretence and abuses but I didn't waver and ended up opening a beer. There was nothing wrong with the hearing of the other team members, because as soon as the top came off, they all ran out. 'I told you I set it up', said Greg, and the tops came off a few more bottles. I celebrated well into the night, thinking that, at last, I was a permanent member of the Australian team again.

Ross Edwards played out the first over the next morning and then I was awakened smartly by the appearance of Bob Willis charging in again. His first delivery was quick. I did see it but couldn't get the bat near it. 'Come on Dougie, for Christ's sake, snick it', he sledged. When he came charging in the second time, the ball landed about the same place and I did snick it, straight to second slip. I trudged back to the dressing room this time, I didn't run. I made it up the steps and met Ian at the door. I just said, 'Don't put off till tomorrow what you can do yesterday', and he didn't comment this time.

My next real high wasn't until 1977 when we were touring New Zealand. My form had tapered off a little, when Dick Tucker, a journalist on the tour, said that he was worried because I'd become only a 50-scorer now. The next Test match in Christchurch I was the last man out for 250, my highest Test score. Many of my team-mates enjoyed telling Dick that he'd got the 50 part right. World Series Cricket then came and went in the next two seasons, and once again I was sitting on the sidelines.

I was back again in 1980–81. This season proved to be my last, even though I'd topped the averages in the Tests against India and New Zealand. I'd practised hard on my technique and changed it a little with the thought in mind that a fifth tour of England may eventuate. However, the final blow was delivered when the team to tour England in 1981 was announced. After waiting anxiously for them to come to the 'Ws', the only name I heard was Wellham, no Walters.

I'd had a pretty good innings so I decided that would do me, but I do often wonder how I would have gone in England if I had been chosen. I guess I had been given enough chances. These days I'm often reminded of my failures in England in the Test matches because I didn't score a century in four tours there. I didn't come to grips with English wickets. They were too slow for my liking and I found that the ball seamed around a lot more on the uncovered wickets.

Another thing was that I think the English captains did their homework and worked out my weaknesses, so the combination of these things led to my undoing. I did score three 80s in Tests in England. Had these become hundreds the story might have been different. I still say that I played some of my best cricket in England, but that was against county teams and didn't really count. Nowadays a good English wicket is as good as any other wicket you will encounter anywhere else in the world, so I might have missed out on a few opportunities.

On reflection, I really don't think there is one thing I would change. If I could have my career over again, and could have exactly the same results, I would be a very happy man and well satisfied with the way it has worked out.

At this stage of my life, I am extremely proud to have my own stand at the SCG as well as a couple of others around the countryside, including one in Dungog. To think that people rated me and my cricket ability highly enough to honour me in this way is very satisfying indeed.

FOUR DUCKS AND A
DEBUT CENTURY

*'Without question the so called "Bookie Scandal" has
been my all-time off-field low and possibly the lowest point
in my life.'*

I've had a fairly steady career. I try not to get too high or too
low. If you're going to succeed at the top, you have to be level-
headed and take a calm approach to the game. If you have
a bad day you can't get too down, and if you have a good
day you can't become too overconfident or full of yourself
because you can rest assured you'll be brought down to earth
pretty quickly.

The guys who don't succeed in the game are often too emotional. They go up and down too much. You have to know how
to move on to the next challenge and not dwell on a day's
events, whether good or bad. That's not to say I haven't had my

moments of both highs and lows during my career. Being the sort of person I am, I prefer to start with the highs.

My Test debut, the fourth Test of the 1990–91 series versus England, would probably be the most thrilling part of my career. I'm sure it would be the same for most of the guys. In Adelaide that day of my debut I made 116 not out, and went on to make 138, and I guess that was a fantastic start. A dream start. It couldn't have been any better. At the same time I was selected, Stephen was dropped from the side, so in one sense it was a high and low point rolled into one for the family and especially for Stephen and me.

Stephen was the one who told me I'd been selected, and my first question was, 'Who's been dropped?' He said, 'I have'. That was hard.

I remember mum and dad were with us, so they were happy for me but sad for Stephen. It was a good lesson for both of us about how professional sports operates. You have to get on with it and not worry about what might have been. It sounds selfish but in the end you have to worry about yourself most of all. You now have an enormous new responsibility. I couldn't do anything about Stephen being dropped but I did have control over how I was going to play. The point is, you control what you can and let everything take its natural course.

Naturally I was still disappointed for Stephen but deep down I have to admit I was very excited about my selection. It would have been great if we'd both made it, but at least one of us was there. If my brother was dropped it was best that I took his place. We're not overly close but when it comes to team selection we obviously feel for each other.

My first 100 was actually my highest point—initially the selection, but then getting the century as well, that was amazing. You never forget your first game but when you make 100 it is even bigger and more memorable. I thought at the time, 'This is too easy. Why didn't they select me years ago?

It's not that hard, this game!' I've learned since it can get a whole lot harder, and then some.

That early success may have lulled me into a false sense of security because I was dropped a year later. In those early days I had the idea that it was just a matter of turning up and making runs, but of course it was much harder than that. It was a great time for me but in the end it wasn't so great. It all came too easily and I didn't work hard enough. It took me a while to realise I had to really work at it.

In my first game, though, I wasn't thinking about any of those things. I just went out and played, very excited just to be there. From that incredible high point I started to worry about making runs and whether I'd keep my place in the side. I started to worry about playing badly. Once you've got more experience, you're more aware of what could go wrong. So I went from that early enjoyment in simply playing, to understanding all too well the pressures of professional sport.

Those pressures can really interfere with your natural game. Talent alone does not guarantee success. You need a whole kit of mental skills and strengths as well. There are so many more things rushing through your mind. What do people think about the way I'm batting? Will I lose my spot? There are so many other good players around—do I measure up? Will I make runs today? When you first get selection, you're so happy to be there, but it soon becomes full on and you have to learn to control all of these new elements.

Of course there were more high points and great moments to come. In the West Indies in Jamaica in 1995 when we beat them 2–1, I made a century and Stephen made 200. We'd always been given a hiding by the West Indies ever since I'd been playing and it was wonderful to beat them in a Test series and contribute to that win. That was the best feeling.

When the team celebrates the high points, the way we celebrate depends on where we are and what's available. We usually stay in the dressing room for a few hours after a Test win. We do all the expected stuff like patting each other on the back and telling each other how good we are and drowning anybody in reach with our drinks. It's such a feeling of relief if it has been hard fought and narrowly won. The captain does his media interviews so we're all just in the room having a drink with the team. Then we sing the team song 'Under the Southern Cross', which is only sung when we win.

Everyone has to leave the dressing room before the team sings the song except for the players and the support staff. David Boon passed the song onto Ian Healy. I think Rod Marsh passed it to Boonie. Whenever we won, Boonie would get up and sing the song and we'd all have a drink and sing along. It's part of our ritual. Heals has passed it on to Ricky Ponting for the one-dayers. Fortunately over the years, 'Under the Southern Cross' has been heard at some point on most tours around the world.

If the game finishes in the middle of the day the celebrations can go on for a long time. We always have our favourite music on a ghetto blaster. Cold Chisel is always played. Stephen always wants John Williamson. It is usually Australian music. When you're overseas it makes you think of home and pretty proud to be playing for your country. INXS, Daryl Braithwaite, Paul Kelly, the Mentals and the Radiators are also very popular among the team.

So we're there with our music, singing and spraying champagne. Then we go back to our hotel rooms before we all go out together. We would never separate on the night of a win. Perhaps we'll have a meal at a club, or go on a harbour cruise if we're in Sydney.

We do get a bit sick of each other on long tours, but when we've won, we definitely want to stick with each other. It's usually the captain's job to decide what sort of celebration we're going to have. If we're in Pakistan there isn't very much you can do so we all go back to someone's room for a few drinks, or to the Australian High Commission. In England and South Africa the celebrations are much bigger.

In 1997 when we beat South Africa in Port Elizabeth in the second Test and I'd made 100, it was a great victory. We had been 188 runs behind at one stage and they had 10 wickets left. We bowled them out. We needed 270 to win but the wicket was very hard to bat on and we got the runs in the fourth innings, so it was a dramatic chase. South Africa were one of the best teams with a quality bowling attack, so winning there was a fantastic high point too. To come from behind and beat them, with Ian Healy hitting a six to win the game, was memorable. There was a lot of tension towards the end of the game. We had an enormous celebration that night. Sometimes you can sit in the dressing room for too long and it's a relief to get out and go home, but that night in Port Elizabeth was different.

Matthew Hayden and Jason Gillespie likened the game to hunting a wild pig and eventually slaying it. They acted out the whole hunting scene in the dressing room. They were dressed up like hunters with ripped shirts and zinc cream on their faces. Matthew Hayden was crawling around on the floor as if he was hunting the pig. He was yelling out and moving through all the spilt beer and cups and other rubbish. Being a country boy Matthew Hayden knew all the moves involved in hunting animals. Eventually he acted out the killing. That was pretty unusual but it shows how powerful the feelings can be.

I'd say we celebrate more than most teams. I remember when England beat us at The Oval, for example, they had one drink after the game and went home. They did have a county game the next day, but still, that looked pretty ordinary from where we stood. I think it is important to stick together and celebrate the wins. It helps our team spirit and is all part of letting off steam at the end of a series.

In marked contrast to those high points and great moments, there are the inevitable lows. Getting four ducks in a row in

Sri Lanka in 1992–93 was an almighty low point. That was probably the lowest point of my career. It was beyond belief. I had never made so many successive low scores in cricket. After I got the fourth duck, I threw all my gear out, giving it to the room attendant.

I thought, 'That's it! I'm bloody well going to retire.' I was semi-serious. I gave him every last bit of my gear. I went home with nothing. No pads, no gloves, no shoes. After that we had about two months off and I gradually forgot about it. I had been very, very distressed. I couldn't believe I could get four ducks because I'd been going really well before that series. I just kept wondering how on earth I'd ever get a run again. I just couldn't get a run.

Mentally I was gone. I remember the third of the ducks, when I was clean bowled. Normally when you get clean bowled you walk straight off, but on this occasion I stood at the crease for about five seconds. I thought I heard the umpire call no-ball, but in actual fact it was the bowler grunting at delivery point. My level of concentration and mind focus were shot ducks, if you'll pardon the pun.

After my two months off I started the season here with NSW and I made a lot of runs. I made 200 against the West Indies in a first-class game and then I was picked for the first Test. So the four ducks was a very low point, but you do bounce back. You have to bounce back.

Other low points would be when I have been dropped. Geoff Marsh and I were dropped playing India in the Perth Test in 1992. Then in 1993 I was dropped in New Zealand for the third Test over there and that was extremely disappointing. When you're dropped you wonder how you'll ever come back. Nearly every player has been dropped at some point so it's not as though you're the first one to go through the experience. That's how you have to look at it. You put your head down and work hard, but it's still a tough situation. You must believe in your ability. There's an old saying that I like and try to hang onto: 'Form is temporary. Class is permanent.'

When we lost the World Cup final in Pakistan against Sri Lanka in 1996 we had really expected to win. We'd been very confident and the World Cup is such a big event, so to lose was extremely disappointing. I didn't make any runs, although I'd played well in the tournament. I hate not contributing. We'd come from nowhere in the semi-final to beat the West Indies. We assumed we'd win because we'd come from so far behind. It was almost like we were fated to win the cup having turned the whole tournament around for ourselves.

A party had been organised for after the game at the home of someone from the High Commission. It was to go ahead whether we won or lost. Naturally you don't feel like going anywhere after a loss, but about five of us fronted up and the rest of the guys stayed at the hotel and went to bed. There's a very big difference between winning and losing, and the atmosphere really pervades the camp. It was difficult trying to mix at the party and maintain conversation with the other guests. Not winning the World Cup when it seemed to be within our reach was a real low.

Without question the so called 'Bookie Scandal' has been my all-time off-field low and possibly the lowest point in my life. The intense pressure and embarrassment following the breaking of the story about Warnie and me taking money from a so called Indian bookmaker cannot be overstated. I simply couldn't believe the storm that raged around us. I was obviously very naive.

At the best of times, I hate media attention. I have always tried to steer clear of it and keep a low profile. Then, all of a sudden, I'm on the front page of every newspaper for supposedly doing something really terrible. It was such an onslaught! I was in Adelaide when it all happened. I didn't want to leave the hotel room. I was constantly worrying about what people were thinking of me—the worst, I know. I felt everyone was staring at me, and they were. Mostly I felt very, very bad for my family. My fiancée, Sue, was with me the whole time, otherwise I don't know how I would have coped.

Dad runs a newsagency and the last thing he wanted to do was sell newspapers with me plastered all over the front of them in such a bad light. My grandmother was very upset about what was being written about me. The family really copped a bit of stick and it was incredible the way they supported me through the whole ordeal.

I had heard rumours in Pakistan that the story was going to appear in the newspapers. I genuinely thought it would all be over in a couple of days because I was looking at it from my perspective, which was that I'd made a stupid mistake several years ago and I'd already paid a penalty and learned the lesson. I knew there was nothing sinister in the whole affair. We'd been incredibly stupid and deserved to be fined and reprimanded but we're not criminals or cheats. I've always given one hundred percent for my country in every game and wouldn't ever consider doing anything less. That was how we were brought up, to always give your best. It is ingrained in us. End of story.

It was very tough walking out onto the field in Adelaide for the first time after the story appeared. I didn't want the bloke before me to ever get out. I didn't want to go in to bat. I wanted to go to bed and sleep. Walking out onto the oval was one of the most difficult things I've ever had to do in my career. I got quite a few boos on the first day. I believe it was mostly the Barmy Army but there were some Aussies booing too. I'd never been booed in my life. Most people like the way I play, so the criticism and the anger of the crowd was a whole new experience and, I can tell you, I didn't like it!

The second innings was better. I got 50-odd. I don't know how I did, but I did. It was very hard to settle in. The Barmy Army were right into me. They were calling me a cheat and you could hear it as plain as day. I don't know how they arrived at the point that I was a cheat—whatever else I might have done. The whole affair had nothing to do with cheating no matter which way you look at it. But they went on and on calling out 'Cheat!' You wouldn't be human if you didn't notice it. Trying to concentrate on the batting was pretty taxing. You can always hear the Barmy Army out in the middle but I am usually able to blank them out. Not that day though. During the first innings I heard every word.

Amazingly, at that lowest point, I played pretty well. I think it was a good lesson. There was so much going on in my life and so much to worry about that I didn't worry about my game. I just went out and played. I was in neutral. I'm sure your natural ability takes over. I made 50, and then in the fifth Test I made 100. It's difficult to explain but I'm sure my play at that point was instinctive. I wasn't worried about how to play shots, I was just worried about getting through the day.

Although the highs far outweigh the lows in my career, I'd be very happy never to go through the sort of grief I experienced in that terrible period ever again.

CHAPTER TWO

THE MILESTONES

COWS, CRICKET AND CIGARETTES

'I only went to school to play sport'

I was born on 21 December 1945 in a hospital in Dungog, NSW, approximately 200 kilometres (124 miles) north of Sydney. My parents disagreed on my name. My mother wanted Kevin and my father wanted Doug. The compromise was that Kevin Douglas is on my birth certificate, but I have always been called Doug. I have an elder brother, Warren, a sister, Colleen, who is a couple of years older than me, and a younger brother, Terry.

As my father worked in timber mills around the area, I spent all my early years in places surrounding the town of Dungog. Living anywhere from ten to twenty kilometres out of town, we had to rely on the local milk pick-up truck to get us to school in most places. There was only one pick-up a day, however, so

23

we often had to walk home. The milk trucks also brought our mail, the paper, bread, meat and many other requirements. Our walk home from school varied from about three to ten kilometres. From about fourth class we upgraded to pushbikes and I fully understand the word 'push', as we did that with our bikes more often than not. We were always repairing punctures, broken chains and the rest. Our brakes weren't the best either— we had to wear out our shoes to stop.

Never a keen scholar, I only went to school to play sport. Athletics, cricket and tennis were our only choices but I was happy as long as I was playing some form of sport when school didn't get in the way.

My other joy as a child was fishing—something I still enjoy. We caught mullet and perch in the local Williams River and some days we caught enough to feed everyone. Mullet is still my favourite fish to eat although many people would only use them for bait. For pocket money we set rabbit traps around various properties, earning five shillings for a pair of carcasses and fair money for the skins. Morning and night we would do the rounds of our traps, sometimes up to 50. With no television or video games, we only went inside the house to eat, sleep or listen to our favourite radio programs, like *Dad and Dave* or *Bob Dyer's Pick a Box* if there was no cricket being broadcast.

Getting electricity was a big event in our lives as it meant an end to searching around for lamps. To have real light and power was great because we could then have a power radio and we didn't have to replace batteries. It's funny how the batteries always seemed to run out at a crucial time.

My father moved for a time from sawing timber to cutting timber in the bush. I was very interested in this and would spend days with him cutting down trees and getting the draught horses to snig them out. I became good at getting the trees to fall where I wanted and giving the right commands to the horses. Chainsaws were not around, and a sharp axe was important.

When tractors replaced the horses I had to learn to drive. I was still only eight or nine but had to become a skillful driver as it could be dangerous on the mountains where we worked.

Progressing to high school and moving onto a dairy farm was the next step. At this time we were 21 kilometres out of town and three kilometres past the end of the line for the milk truck. The 5,300 hectare property (13,000 acres) was owned by the people my father worked for in the timber mills and cutting the timber. They had cleared enough of the property to run cattle but there was still a lot of bush. One paddock was 2,500 hectares, so the cows took a lot of finding sometimes.

We had no electricity there for another two years and although we had a diesel motor to do our milking, it didn't always start. When it failed, everyone had to get in and work because it was hard to milk 180 cows by hand twice a day. Our milk pick-up, three kilometres down the road, was at 6.30am so early starts like 3.00am became normal. I used to help milk a few cows then have breakfast and get changed for school ready for our ride on the milk truck to where we could meet the bus.

High school and different teachers was hard for me to cope with. I couldn't wait until the Intermediate Certificate in third year was over. My sport improved, though, with high school. We even had basketball and soccer as well as the other sports I had been playing in primary school. But my main love was still cricket. I was having success, mainly with the ball, but also scoring runs which I was marking down on the back of my bat (rather than drawing 'stick' people on my thigh pad like my co-author does). In fact I didn't know what a thigh pad was in those days. My batting gloves, which I rarely wore, had pimples, not sausages, on them. My junior cricket in Dungog and later Maitland was very successful.

Back on the farm the cows were becoming very boring. We knew every cow by name, which bail she would go in, and any other of her habits. I took to the other side of dairying, preferring to plough fields and grow crops. I could get on the tractor and go all day and into the night if that meant I didn't have to get up and milk those cows—which I often did.

School finally finished and I worked on the dairy for a couple of years. Then came my big decision. If my cricket career was going to go any further then I had to move. The invitation to move to Sydney had already come after I had played two Sheffield Shield matches when I was 17. However, NSW had a very good side so I needed to play grade cricket every week if I wanted the selectors to notice me. I really had no other choice. It certainly was a big step, moving to a big city from a quiet farm three kilometres from your nearest neighbour.

Cumberland was my new cricket club and they arranged a place for me to board. They also found me a new job. I boarded with the parents of one of the Cumberland players. He was married and no longer lived there but I had the company of his younger brother, Sid, who was a bit older than me. The Goodwins' home was in Wentworthville, in western Sydney, relatively close to the Cumberland home ground. The family treated me as one of their own. They were as good as their name suggested. I was warned, however, not to keep company with Sid because he liked to go to the club, and that wouldn't help my cricket. I was a non-drinker then so the club (Wentworthville Leagues) didn't have a great deal of appeal for me anyway. In those days you had to be 21 before you could go into licensed clubs, even if you only drank lemon squash.

My new job was with a wholesale grocery chain in Homebush, which is now near the Sydney Olympics site. I worked from 7.30am to 4.00pm and caught a train there and back. I never enjoyed getting out of bed early but I'd had to get up earlier when I lived on the farm. However, packing grocery trolleys and loading them onto trucks became as tedious as the cows after a short time. I didn't want to complain too soon, so stuck it out for three months until the cricket season started again. I then let them know that I would prefer something else, preferably a sports store.

It didn't take too long before I had a job with another wholesale company, called Grimleys. They were on Broadway in the city and sold just about everything. I started in the toy department then worked my way up to the sports section. The toy department wasn't bad, but I wished I'd had those toys as a child. Grimleys were very good to me. They gave me time off for practice twice a week and they also gave me time off to play for NSW and then Australia for a short time. They even sold my first autographed bats and pads under a brand called Sportsmaster. I must admit that I did push some of those sales because I was on an incentive scheme for the number sold. For bats sold with my autograph, I got two shillings for a senior and one shilling for a junior. (My wage was £6 a week and the bats sold for around £16.) Sales picked up with my success in the Australian team.

After two years with Grimleys other job offers came my way and Rothmans was to become my next employer. They offered a company car which would be renewed annually. This really appealed to me because my first car, a Mini Minor which I had bought new, had now done more than 100,000 miles (161,000 kilometres). They also offered time off for practice games and tours. I was a non-smoker which I told them, but that was okay as long as I carried cigarettes on my person and offered them to other people, they would continue to pay me while I was on leave for cricket commitments. Like many kids, I had tried smoking at school, but it didn't appeal to me at all then.

I had only been at Rothmans for a matter of weeks when I was called up for National Service training. I had started to enjoy a drink by this time, but had still not been tempted to smoke. I had actually tried one during a shopping-centre promotion. I offered a cigarette from a new brand packet to a person and lit it for him. This person said, 'Doug, they can't be too good if you're not going to have one'. I thought on this for a short while, then also lit up. I didn't enjoy this any more than I had done at school, in fact I started coughing, and smoke came out of my ears, nose, eyes, everywhere. I still have visions of this person laughing as I sought to stamp the cigarette out after that one puff.

I didn't like having to go into National Service. Many of the other young recruits felt the same, but it wasn't any use complaining. I was given a pretty hard time to begin with, being one of the first well-known sportsmen to be enlisted. I felt that they made me an example for everyone else. Whenever a volunteer was needed for anything, my name was called out first. The first six weeks were the worst, with no leave outside the barracks and no drinking. My cigarette deliveries still came from Rothmans though. I was very popular with the other recruits because I had no use for the cigarettes myself and kept many others supplied. This lasted for about six months before I tried another puff. By this time we had settled into the army routine and had access to a mess which had a bar. While we were up at the mess one night I tried another cigarette and got through it without too much coughing. This led to one or two a day and, before long, the other recruits were buying their own cigarettes.

I got married during my second year of National Service. Caroline and I had gone to school together in Dungog, although it wasn't until after we left school that our relationship blossomed. Caroline had moved from Dungog around the time I was doing my training and worked as a teacher at Wentworthville. After we were married we lived in a unit in Wentworthville, not far from where I had been boarding. Having Caroline with me helped me get through my National Service. My training finally came to an end and I went back to Rothmans, cricket and a normal life. At least I hadn't been sent to Vietnam, and I was still alive. Some of my friends, and a lot of others, had not been so lucky. The way I accepted these two years and many other umpiring decisions has helped me through life and business.

I left Rothmans after 15 years. Life continues long after cricket, although my present business activities are centred on the game. We now have four children, three boys and a girl, three of them born since my retirement from cricket. I do a lot of after-dinner speaking, a lot of coaching and some work promoting City Index. City Index is an interesting betting system, allowing the individual to be the bookie and bet on individuals and team performances, rather than on the outcome of the race or match. Index betting is quite new in Australia, but it is very popular overseas and I think it will grow here when people understand it more. I hope to be able to help them understand the way it works, as it becomes an increasing part of my future.

SPORT, SPORT AND SPORT

'We played a memorable first game in which we both made ducks and contributed absolutely nothing in the field except for building sandcastles at fine-leg.'

My life officially started at 8.18pm on 2 June 1965. I was born the younger twin by four minutes to my brother Stephen at Canterbury Hospital in Sydney. Mum tells us we were our uncle's tenth birthday present. It must have been very cosy inside my mum's belly, and having come out some 1.8 kilograms (4 pounds) heavier than Stephen it is clear who had been getting the lion's share of the available food and nourishment.

My middle name is Edward, after my dad's father. I have three brothers including Stephen. The others, Dean and Daniel, are some three-and-a-half and ten years younger than me, respectively.

I believe I was very lucky to be brought up in a sport-oriented

31

family, with mum and dad both junior state tennis champions. I think sport is just in our blood. Mum and dad originally met through their sport. They were married at the age of 18 and then had us twins soon after.

What a shock it must have been at the age of 19, when starting their own careers, to also have the responsibility of bringing up twins. When I think about that I realise what an incredible struggle it must have been—one that I don't know I could cope with now let alone at the age of 19.

I think dad could easily have been a professional tennis player, having been equally as good as Tony Roche, Phil Dent and Mark Edmondson. He did play in the NSW Open one year, in the doubles with his good friend Tony Musgrove, against a reasonably well-known player called Ken Rosewell and a Russian, Alex Metrevilli. Dad and Tony were beaten but I still clearly remember watching the contest.

Each long weekend in Easter and October for about ten years we would travel to Gloucester and Taree, where mum and dad would play in their respective tennis tournaments. Stephen, Dean and I would spend all day playing soccer, cricket and tennis on any spare bit of grass behind the courts. We were pretty well obsessed with sport by then.

Dad worked in the National Bank for more than twenty years before moving into his newsagency business and he did a bit of private tennis coaching too. Mum has been a trained school teacher all her life and is also a swimming instructor to underprivileged children.

From when we were about three years old, I can remember dad hitting tennis balls to Stephen and myself in the backyard. If we didn't catch them we wore them. My first official sporting competition was playing T-Ball for East Hills in the maroon and white colours, and then came soccer for the Milperra Lions.

Cricket was soon to follow and we debuted at six years of age for the under-10s at Panania/East Hills. We played a memorable first game in which we both made ducks and contributed absolutely nothing in the field except for building sandcastles at fine-leg. I do, however, remember placing the box on the inside of my knee and then in the back of my trousers. So you could say all was looking promising from an early age.

At this stage I was a student at Panania Infants and then Panania Primary School. I was a steady student rather than a brilliant one but I wasn't averse to school and did enjoy some aspects of the academic side of things too.

We were quite soon into rep cricket, playing for Bankstown in the Foster's Shield under-10s. Improvement from my first game was quite rapid and by the end of primary school, soccer, cricket and tennis took up most of my time, and most of mum and dad's as well.

That year was very busy because Stephen and I both made the state team in all three codes. Back then we lived in a modest and comfortable house in Panania where footballs and tennis and golf balls often flew onto neighbours' roofs, into gardens and sometimes through windows. In those days mum was the one who would drive the blue Holden more miles than the Leyland Brothers to and from training and matches, while dad was busy working in town.

High school was soon upon us and East Hills Boys High was the next stepping stone. I found it to be a top school which was strong on sport but also quite strict. It was a school at which you could develop academically but it also encouraged you to play sport and certainly didn't restrict you in trying out for rep teams or playing sport during school hours.

The three boys, Stephen, Dean and myself, certainly tested the teachers' patience and I clearly remember being late for school nearly every day. Trying to get three teenage boys who loved sleeping-in off to school together was a nightmare for mum and we would often rock up midway through the first lesson at about 9.30.

Towards the end of high school, at the age of about 17, our cricket and soccer were beginning to overlap. Playing first-grade cricket with Bankstown Canterbury and playing second-grade soccer with Bankstown then Sydney Croatia was getting too hectic. Cricket was my greater love and I was probably better at it anyway. Soccer had to go.

Bankstown Canterbury District Cricket Club was a club rich in tradition and a good breeding ground for Australian players—like Len Pascoe, Jeff Thomson, Ian Davis and Steve Smith who had all been through the Bankstown cricket grade scene.

Once school finished, Australia under-19s and Sheffield Shield selection followed quickly. I didn't have much money and I didn't have a full-time job apart from going to England to play a season with Bolton in the Lancashire League immediately after finishing high school. I did have a few part-time jobs including indoor cricket umpiring, packing (and sleeping in) boxes at ML sporting goods, and working as a sales rep at Kingsgrove Sporting Centre with my good friend Harry Solomons. This is when I first met Susan, my fiancée, and we've lived together ever since. It is also when I bought my first car, a dark blue Sigma. It was great to finally have a car I didn't have to share with Stephen—which also meant I didn't have to worry about it running out of petrol.

Since the early days of representing NSW in cricket, my life has become very busy, playing cricket all around the world and fulfilling commitments for my many supportive sponsors. Playing cricket for your country is a huge honour but it also means you are public property. Every move you make on and off the field is monitored. It takes a level head and a bit of give-and-take to make life run smoothly.

My personal manager, Leo Karis, has been a great help to me through all the good and bad times and he has played a big role in keeping my current sponsors happy and in creating new opportunities for me in the corporate world. Companies like

Dunlop, Slazenger, Toyota, Bollé, Nizoral and 2UE have all worked with me and been very supportive. After cricket who knows what I will do, but I would think it will have something to do with sport and probably cricket.

CHAPTER THREE

THE CAPTAINCY

SPECIAL SKILLS REQUIRED FOR TOP JOB

'Richie had an enormous influence on my cricket when I was a child. The way he captained Australia had a lot to do with the way I played cricket.'

I believe that great captains are born that way. It is not a learned skill, and it is the same in business—some people seem to fall on their feet no matter what they turn their hand to, whereas others can never reach the same levels. I dare say that some politicians also fit into this category.

Captaincy is probably the only change I would make if I could have my career over again. At a young age, I was pushed into taking on the captaincy of my club side, Cumberland (now called Parramatta). This was mainly because I was playing for NSW and I was expected to have more experience than the other members of my team. I went to a couple of club selection meetings because captains were automatically selectors as well. At these meetings, they would pick the five grade sides as well as a city and suburban side. At this stage I only knew both names of about half the first-grade players and I had never ever seen the players in the other grades, let alone know their names.

When I moved to Cumberland from Dungog, I had already played two games for NSW so I went straight into the Cumberland first-grade side without moving up from the juniors, as most other players in the area would. I chose to move to Cumberland because Richie Benaud was the Australian captain at that stage and he was also the Cumberland captain. As soon as Richie retired, I was made captain, and I found it very difficult, even unfair, to select players from scores alone. I soon opted out of selection meetings, feeling that there were many with better qualifications to do that job.

After playing for NSW for a few seasons, I was urged to take on the state captaincy. I wasn't exactly putting up my hand and asking for the job but it was handed to me anyway. I guess I did enjoy the challenge it offered for a few seasons, but I wasn't disappointed when I was relieved of that task. I don't actually think it affected my play as much as it did others', but I did enjoy playing my cricket much more when I didn't have the extra worries. Some people automatically take it in their stride, and I think they are people who really want the job.

These days I guess captains, and coaches too, live and die by the results of their team. I don't think this should be the case. Coaches, in particular, can't go onto the field and produce a good innings, or a number of wickets or catches to pull their team out of trouble. However, if a team is not performing consistently, the coach is the first person who is blamed. The captain is the next person in line as blame is apportioned.

The job is very rewarding while a team is playing well, and great captains can make this happen. In past years the English captain has been selected first, and then teams have been chosen around this captain. I don't think this method always works because if a captain is not worthy of his place in the team because of his ability with either the bat or the ball, he needs a lot of good results to earn, and then maintain, the respect of his team-mates.

I prefer the method used in Australia whereby a team is picked on ability and then a captain is selected from within that team. This happens at all levels of cricket in Australia. I felt very lucky to have played under one of the all time great cricket captains, Richie Benaud, when I first arrived in Sydney, but to take over once he left was not as easy as it might sound. It could be likened to scoring a century in your first Test match. Everyone expects that you can only get better with every innings after that. Unfortunately, there is often only one way to go from there, and that is down. Richie did teach me a lot of tricks. These helped me not only on the field of play, but off as well.

In order, the Test captains I played under were Brian Booth, Bob Simpson, Bill Lawry, Barry Jarman, Ian Chappell and Greg Chappell. Brian Booth only captained Australia a couple of times, filling in for Bob Simpson, and Barry Jarman filled in once when Bill Lawry was injured in England in 1968. All captains have their own personalities, and all of these captains did a good job in their own way, but I felt that some were better and more successful than others for different reasons.

I was disappointed not to have played under Richie Benaud for either NSW or Australia, but I did enjoy my matches for Cumberland under his captaincy, and I still rate him as equal to the best captains I have seen. I actually played a couple of Sheffield Shield games with Richie in the NSW side, but because of his impending retirement he had handed over the captaincy to Bob Simpson.

Richie had an enormous influence on my cricket when I was a child. The way he captained Australia had a lot to do with the way I played cricket. No one could possibly forget the famous 1960–61 series against the West Indies. It took two great captains to generate the quality of cricket during that series, and I guess it took two great teams as well. I can recall Richie being adventurous as a captain before that series as well. He had a manner that gave me a feeling of awe. This was, and is, both on and off the cricket field, and I think if opposing batsmen felt the same they could be out before they even batted. He still has enormous respect from all his team members as well as opposing teams, and I think this makes him a truly great captain.

I also think of Ian Chappell in much the same way as I do Richie. I'm sure that Richie also influenced Ian as a youngster and Ian learned many tactics from him. Ian also admired Richie, and he still has this great respect for him. I have had many long conversations with Ian about captaincy. From the time Ian took over the captaincy of Australia he changed markedly, and initially this was hard to understand. I wasn't the only one who had trouble coming to terms with the change— many other team members felt the same as well.

Prior to the captaincy job, Ian had been one of the boys, always one of the last to leave the bar, but once he was appointed captain he was suddenly one of the first to leave. I found it hard to comprehend but then his reasons became more obvious. He needed to be the one to set the example and by doing this he gained more respect from everyone. This reason alone would be enough to discourage me from wanting the job.

I didn't ever want to captain any team. While Ian may not have been in the bars in person, he did know exactly who was there and for how long. I don't think he actually minded Rod Marsh and myself being there but he wasn't too impressed if he saw some of our other players there for too long and soon let them know that he wasn't amused. Most players know what they can or can't do, but Ian was always just around the corner to guide you in the right direction. Prior to departing on one tour, I can remember Ian stating to the team, 'If anyone has any problems either on or off the field, just remember, my door is always open'. Marshie and I took him up on this offer a couple of times and spent a long time in his room explaining our 'off the field' problems. The hotel bars shut very early in some places and Rod and I felt it was necessary to check on the captain's fridge to see if he could help in those particular situations.

It was great to know a captain in this way. He put himself out for the sake of the players, more often than many people ever knew. He continually argued for better pay and conditions for his players. I'm sure that the players understood this and they, in turn, gave him an extra ten percent of effort on the playing field. Ian understood cricket very well but I think he understood cricketers even better.

A lot of good captains do the job very well between 11.00am and 6.00pm, the cricket playing hours, but fall down on their job outside these hours. Ian Chappell could never be accused of captaining in this way. Of course I never played under the captaincy of Mark Taylor but I would rate Mark right up with Richie and Ian. I was impressed with Mark Taylor from the very first time he captained Australia and felt that he improved match by match. I also think that his decision to retire when he did was excellent. He showed impeccable timing. It is always better to quit while you're on top and, more importantly, while Australian cricket was on top.

Mark's record speaks for itself. He was prepared to take the risks and his players always responded. He was a 'hands on' captain. Mark took on jobs that in today's game are often left to the coach. He not only handled his players well, but he also did an outstanding job with the media.

Bob Simpson was my first full-time Test captain. He did the job when the Australian team was in a rebuilding phase. Bill Lawry took over from Simpson and he was in a similar situation as Australia struggled during those years. The Australian selectors eventually dropped Bill, and Ian Chappell was given the captaincy job. The sacking was not popular in many circles. I felt there was a case for making Ian captain, but Bill not only lost the captaincy, he was dropped from the team as well.

Bill may not have been rated as a great captain, but at the time he was dropped I felt he was the best opening batsman in Australia. Bob Simpson and Bill Lawry were a great opening pair and I think it is doubtful that Australia has ever had a better combination.

Greg Chappell was the final Test captain I played under. He also captained a team when there were problems with team changes, as it was after World Series Cricket, and taking over from his brother, Ian, was not an easy job. Greg's initial team consisted of mostly the same players Ian had captained. However, the team was not as successful, and I feel that this shows my original point to be correct—that great captains are born, and captaincy is not a skill that can be learned.

My biggest mistake as captain was when I was captain of Cumberland. We were playing against Petersham Marrickville in an all-day game. The scheduled hours of play were 10.00am to 6.00pm. The match was to be played on Merrylands Oval. Merrylands had a pretty good wicket, and a very fast outfield. I won the toss and did not hesitate in deciding that we would bat first. We got off to a good start, and I closed the innings just after lunch at no wicket for 319 runs. I thought that should keep our opposition busy. We were at the Billabong Hotel, five kilometres away, by 5.30pm and this was after showering and changing. Needless to say, we lost the match.

No Petersham batsman scored a hundred that day. One actually should have, but when they passed our score, the Petersham captain, Noel Hughes, suggested that we should play on until Brian Riley, who was on 99, at the time, scored his century. I wasn't exactly ecstatic at that stage, but agreed to his suggestion, and pushed all the Cumberland fielders back to the boundary.

I did this so that 'Riles' could score his century without any stress, and the quicker he scored it, the quicker we could get to the Billabong Hotel to drown our sorrows.

Believe it or not, Brian Riley wasn't satisfied to just take the single to score an even hundred. One of his arch-enemies—the very talented off spinner Bob Aitken—was bowling, and Riles' objective was to hit him out of the Merrylands ground and into the swimming pool nearby. He charged down the wicket and had an almighty swing. He was out, clean bowled for 99.

Another grade match that comes readily to mind was when Richie was captain. We were playing at the old Cumberland Oval, now the Parramatta Football Stadium. The match was against Northern Districts. It had rained most of the prior week, and the wicket was quite badly affected. Our batsmen were delighted when Richie won the toss, but when he told us we were batting first, we thought he must have lost the plot somewhere. He told us the wicket was still too wet and the ball would skid off and not pop up as it often does if the wicket is damp. We were bowled out for 49 and we didn't think much of Richie's theory at that stage.

When we took to the field, we found that Richie had another couple of tricks up his sleeve. Firstly, he planned to take the new ball and bowl seamers. I was opening the bowling with him. He walked down the wicket and marked out a big cross on a good length with his sprigs. 'That's where I want you to land them,' he said. We got five for twenty each, and Northern Districts were out for 42. This story is just to add more weight to my opening statement.

Captaincy is a very special role. Deservedly, it can give you the respect of many people, particularly if you captain your national side. However, taking on the captaincy also means that you come under close scrutiny, and the press as well as the public can quickly become very fickle when the national team does not win. A few English captains and, more recently, Brian Lara from the West Indies, have found that they ride a rollercoaster of emotions determined by Test and international one-day match results.

It seems that there is always someone gunning for the captaincy position. Half the time, I think the suggestions of people wanting the captaincy are only media speculation and the quotes are taken out of context, often unsubstantiated and unreliable. When the Australian team recently arrived in the West Indies for the 1999 tour, Shane Warne, the Vice Captain, stepped off the plane after about 72 hours of travel with his tie loosened. The photos of him were instantly sent around the world.

I could hardly believe that this was on the front page of our newspaper, with the caption asking, 'IS THIS MAN FIT TO CAPTAIN OUR COUNTRY? I DON'T THINK SO'. I would really like to have seen a photo of the journalists as they arrived. I'll bet none were wearing ties. I guess English captains have to put up with that kind of negative writing all the time but surely we don't need people like that covering our cricket. The press has buried many English captains over the years, but up until this time our captains have been left fairly well alone. This doesn't mean that the press does not harass our captains. I know from experience it doesn't matter what time of the day or night it is, they will ring, regardless of whether it wakes you up or not. When there are media teams and full-time managers on tour, the pressure on captains is eased a little.

Steve's captaincy during the recent World Cup Series in 1999 was first class, given that he may not have been handed the right team in the earlier games. The Australian fielding for most of these games wasn't up to its usual standard, and these days we do mark hard, but Steve showed his usual confidence in a team that many others had written off. He proved with his bat what makes a good captain. Herschelle Gibbs dropping a simple catch (that it appeared he had taken) proved that luck also plays an important part.

For the first time in my life I had doubts about Shane Warne's ability to win one-day games for Australia but Steve wisely maintained his faith in him, which proves you never knock a champion. Steve Waugh's faith, led from the top, to me shows he has got all it takes to be our next great captain.

A TOUGH JOB BUT SOMEONE HAS TO DO IT

'Allan Border was a captain who occasionally let his frustrations turn into dummy spits. In practice on tour he might walk out if we dropped a few catches in a row just to let us know we were wasting everybody's time.'

The main captains I've played under are Allan Border, Mark Taylor, Geoff Lawson, Shane Warne, Stephen and, of course, Graham Gooch when I was at Essex. It looks like a tough but rewarding job from where I stand, although I've never had the opportunity to captain in first-class cricket myself.

All captains have their different styles. For example, Mark Taylor was very communicative whereas Allan Border wasn't. Mark Taylor was in fact a great communicator. He'd address the players personally and have a bit of an encouraging chat with you. It was often a one-on-one approach and he'd guide you along which made you feel pretty confident about your game.

Allan Border, on the other hand, felt that if you were in the Australian side you were perfectly capable of playing your own game and going along in your own way. He didn't feel it was his job to be constantly telling you what to do. He very much led by example with his own batting and fielding. You certainly wouldn't call him a big talker, but I wouldn't say it was better or worse—just a different approach. He was still a fine captain.

When I played my first Test in Adelaide, Allan Border was captain and I assumed he would talk to me a lot and give me a few tips, generally welcoming me into the team. I thought he might says things like, 'It isn't a lot harder than Shield cricket', or 'You're good enough, you'll make it'. Instead he didn't say anything at all. No comments. No reassurances. It obviously didn't bother me because I made a century! He just let me go for it. Mark Taylor would definitely have spoken to the new guys. He would reassure them that they were in the side because they were good enough and he told you to believe in your own ability.

Allan Border did have a tough time in the early days when he was captain. His team lost for many years. By the time I joined the team, it wasn't his way to talk to individual players a lot. I don't know if that had always been his style. If he did say something, you would certainly listen and learn. Stephen, on the other hand, is more like Mark Taylor. He'll chat to the players individually and guide them along. Geoff Lawson was extremely aggressive as captain and not all that personal with his instructions but I liked his enthusiasm and his positive approach. Gooch was perhaps too gentle. He'd come up and chat in a really quiet way. If anything he was too soft, but I liked playing under him and Essex were very much a winning combination when he was at the helm.

Mark Taylor was the best captain I've played under. Everyone

liked and respected him. He had a great demeanour. He'd
rarely upset and he was a very calming and steadying influence
over the whole team. He made everything simple and clear.
That is great for the guys on the team because if the captain
isn't upset and he's saying it's all okay then you feel it's under
control. We would go out feeling that we were going well as a
team when he was around. I can hardly remember a single
dummy spit when Mark was the captain. He left his dummy
spits to the golf courses around the world, where a bad hook
off the tee would cause him more frustration than one from
his bat.

Allan Border was a captain who occasionally let his frustrations turn into dummy spits. During practice on tour he might
walk out if we dropped a few catches in a row just to let us
know that we were wasting everybody's time. That was more
towards the end of his career, and perhaps he'd just had
enough. When he used to bat in the nets he'd get a little grumpy
if you mucked around. One day in Perth I accidentally bowled
him a bouncer and it nearly hit him. He just hooked it off his
head and I sort of laughed and apologised saying I didn't mean
it, which I didn't. He came straight out of the nets and yelled,
'What the hell are you laughing at? Wipe that smile off your
face right now!' Just little things like that could creep into his
behaviour but it was fairly rare and would blow over pretty
quickly. He might not talk to you the next day but then it was
dropped and never mentioned again. To him it was just part of
the pressured position at the top of cricket, and he would never
hold a grudge against you. It was his way of blowing off steam.

Goochie was just so easy and gentle in comparison. He rarely
yelled at the players and probably didn't come down hard enough
when guys weren't putting in. Warnie, on the other hand, really
likes to rev people up when he's captain. It must come from the
AFL tradition in Victoria. Before we go out he'll yell, 'Come on,
let's go out there and get into them. Let's concentrate'. Mark

Taylor would rarely raise his voice. He'd just quietly say, 'Alright let's go and have a good day'.

Shane talks more than any other player I've played with. His style is very vocal and he's an up-front type. It's definitely the Victorian way—as though he's talking to a football team. That's how Warnie likes to assert his authority. It must be something about the Victorians generally because Merv and Dean Jones were also good talkers. Mind you, Fleming and Reiffel don't say a word. But Warnie will repeat ten times what we're supposed to do, even though we've already discussed it, because it's his way of revving us up.

I think Stephen deserves to be the new captain, as he's shown at the World Cup. He's worked for it and has all the credentials. I would love to have had a chance to be captain and still hope I get a go at being a captain in first class-cricket one day—perhaps for NSW or in England. For me it would be an opportunity to look at cricket from an entirely new angle.

There are many attributes that I think are required of a good captain. First of all, you have to be a good enough player to be picked in the team all the time. I don't agree with what they did in England when they chose Mike Brearley as captain. He was a great captain but couldn't bat. These days I don't think a team can afford to carry a captain who can't play or who isn't really good enough to be in the team. It is of primary importance that the captain is also a good player who makes the team on his merits.

Naturally you've also got to have a strong knowledge of cricket. You have to know the intricacies of the game. You need to have great knowledge of the opposition players and generally be able to develop tactics. You can't just be good at tossing the coin and leading the players around. All the captains I've played under have been good tacticians and they have been very knowledgeable about the game.

You must also have the respect of your team-mates. A captain cannot expect his players to do something he would never do. The captain must be able to lead by example. If you have even a single team member who doesn't respect you and your knowledge, then you've got a problem on your hands. In my time I've never seen that happen.

Most of the guys I've played with over the years have liked the captain, and on a few occasions where they haven't liked the captain personally, they have at least respected him as a cricket captain. You have to be able to respect and accept the captain's decisions and judgement even if you don't agree with the decisions. You might not want to go to dinner with the captain after a game but you must at least be prepared to listen and follow when you're playing. If the captain tells you to do something, you have to do it or you may as well not be there.

The captain must be able to remain level-headed under pressure and carefully weigh up all the options in a short space of time. It is far easier to make decisions when you're not the captain. For example, when I gave an opinion to Mark Taylor, I would think carefully about my answer, but ultimately the real decision was his. Out there in the middle we might all have different opinions about how to best achieve results.

When I was in slips Mark Taylor would often ask what I thought about various things. For example, who should bowl next? Heals, Stephen and I might all say something different so a final decision must be reached by the captain. I don't think it is an easy position to be in. His decision can make all the difference to the direction of the game and sometimes determine whether a game is won or lost. So coolness under pressure is an absolute prerequisite for a successful captaincy. Trusting and using your gut feeling and natural instinct can also be vital. You must have the courage of your convictions.

In one respect the captain is only as good as his team. If he gives someone the ball to have a bowl and they bowl very well and grab a wicket or two, then it could be said that the captain has made an excellent decision, but it could equally be said that the bowler has made the captain look good. It is, however, the captain's job to know his players well and to bring out the strengths of the individuals as well as drawing the guys together as a team. Mark Taylor had a squad of tremendous talent during his reign as Australian captain but he knew how to draw the best out of those individuals.

One of the most difficult parts of the captain's job must be maintaining and concentrating on his own game while also being responsible for the team's performance. The captain still has to bat or, in Geoff Lawson's case, bowl. I remember when Mark Taylor first started out in Karachi he got a pair. He clearly wasn't concentrating on his own game because he was absorbed with the role of captain. This is natural, but good captains quickly adapt and get things in the right perspective.

Usually if your own game is in disarray you'll withdraw from the guys a bit and try to sort things out. You'll be really focused on the problem. If you're the captain you don't have that luxury. So the captain has two equally important jobs, and that is a lot of pressure. It took Mark a few games to sort out the balance between his own game, the team's game, and the media and administrative obligations. Stephen has been going through the same process and I think everyone would agree he is handling it with the utmost professionalism.

It would also be difficult to emerge from a team and a group of peers to take on the captaincy. Suddenly you have to be a bit aloof and a bit distanced from the other guys, many of whom you've known for years. You're now involved in team selections on tour and at home. You have to make hard decisions all the time where good mates are involved. That's not easy but it's the nature of the beast.

You also inherit an immense amount of media work and you're constantly giving interviews at times when you would previously have been training or celebrating or just getting

Cricket wasn't the only sport I participated in as a child, although it did take up most of my time. Here I am (centre, front) showing off my ribbons after an athletics meet in 1955 with some fellow schoolmates at Bandon Grove School in Dungog. *Courtesy: Doug Walters*

Before my Test debut in Brisbane in 1965 with Captain Brian Booth, who was standing in because Bob Simpson had a broken wrist.
Courtesy: News Limited

Just arrived in Sydney fresh from Dungog. I'm carrying a cricket kit bag circa 1963 —a bit different from what Mark carries today. *Courtesy: News Limited*

When I first moved to Sydney, in 1963–64, I kept my eye in during the winter by playing baseball. Here I'm batting for Parramatta City.
Courtesy:
Doug Walters

Leaving the army after two years of National Service training, to join the 1968 tour to England. I decided the creams would be more fun than the khakis.
Courtesy:
News Limited

Signing autographs for local children in Dungog after the official naming of the Doug Walters Pavilion at the local cricket ground on January 15, 1966. *Courtesy: Doug Walters*

With my mother, May, my wife, Caroline, and my father, Ted, at a civic reception which followed the opening of the Pavilion. *Courtesy: Doug Walters*

My performance in Sheffield Shield during the 1972–73 season earned me a place back in the Australian side, after being dropped for the fifth Test in England in August 1972. *Courtesy: News Limited*

I felt very lucky to have played under one of the all-time great cricket captains, Richie Benaud (above), when I first arrived in Sydney.
Courtesy: Ern McQuillan

Proof that I did occasionally go to the nets, although I couldn't really see the point. *Courtesy: Doug Walters*

On my way to a double century against the West Indies, 1968–69. The keeper is Jackie Hendriks and behind him is Roy Fredericks. *Courtesy: Doug Walters*

Surrounded by children after a match at the SCG, November 1970— in the days when people were allowed onto the ground. *Courtesy: The Fairfax Photo Library*

With Ian Chappell, getting ready to tour New Zealand in 1974. He was a terrific captain and gained the respect of everyone. *Courtesy: News Limited*

Arriving at Sydney Airport after the tour to England in 1977. I'm tight-lipped with the media following the announcement of World Series Cricket. *Courtesy: News Limited*

Playing in the World Series Cricket competition. I believe its arrival was the biggest and best change to the game.
Courtesy: Doug Walters

On the way to Royal Ascot with Richie Robinson for the race meeting in 1977. Touring gave us wonderful experiences like this.
Courtesy: News Limited

In the SCG dressing room with Steve Rixon (centre) and Peter Toohey waiting for the rain to clear. It looks like I'm going for misère.
Courtesy: News Limited

On my way to 67 in my last SCG Test innings, 3 January 1981, v India. Australia won by an innings and 4 runs. *Courtesy: The Fairfax Photo Library.*

After World Series Cricket began, Sheffield Shield didn't draw the same crowds, as this shot from the SCG in 1980 shows. *Courtesy: The Fairfax Photo Library*

Test matches (such as this match against India, January 1981, also at the SCG) did maintain a strong following. *Courtesy: The Fairfax Photo Library*

With two more of the captains I played under, at a benefit breakfast held for me in 1981. Bob Simpson (top) and Greg Chappell (bottom).
Courtesy: News Limited

I'm proud to have had cricket stands named after me. Here I am in front
of the original Doug Walters stand at the SCG at my launch for *The Doug
Walters Story* in 1981. *Courtesy: News Limited*

through the airport to the hotel. You're now the public face of the team. If the team starts losing you're the one they'll focus on. Naturally there is a captain's allowance, which is fair enough given the doubled workload and the expectations.

Captaincy is definitely a very difficult role but it can obviously be immensely satisfying. Only the strong of heart and mind can survive and grow in the job. I consider myself fortunate to have played under such great captains—all with different styles but, most importantly, all successful.

CHAPTER FOUR

LIFE ON THE ROAD

MONEY COULDN'T BUY IT

*'Anyway he was a delightful roomy. Not too many others in
the team would have waited up for me to come home.'*

My first overseas tour with the Australian team was in 1968 to
England. The duration of the tour was almost seven months. I
would liken my feelings about my first tour to those I had
before my first Test match, particularly since it was to England
which I looked on as the home of cricket.

At the time of this English tour I had just finished two years
of National Service training. Towards the end of that two years
I was offered an extra few months in the service for an overseas
tour that not too many people wanted to go on. I declined that
offer because the team for the English tour had already been
announced and I knew it would guarantee me a return ticket,
which Vietnam didn't. I also thought the creams sounded much
more enjoyable than the khaki. The army had taken care that

my passport was up-to-date, just in case, so that was one thing I didn't have to do to prepare for the tour.

This tour of England was at a time of change, as it was the first time the Australian team was to fly both ways. In 1964 when the Australian team toured England, the players went by ship to Bombay then flew the rest of the way. It was customary for them to play a match in Tasmania and then another one in Perth before heading off on the ship. The thought of spending six weeks on a ship is enough to make me feel hung over. Can you possibly imagine the kind of records Rod Marsh and I could have set from Perth to London in that time?

The big thing about touring with the Australian team is wondering who you are going to share a room with for that length of time. With the excitement and anticipation of my first tour, I didn't care. Besides that, I had had a minimum of four room-mates for the previous two years. In 1968 there were a number of players touring for the first time. I had eyed off the team and picked my preferences, but it didn't work that way. Bill Lawry was the captain of the team in 1968 and he had a fair say in the rooming arrangements. He had decided that a man called Les Joslin was the ideal person to keep me in shape.

I don't know till this day whether Bill realised that I had changed my lifestyle somewhat in the two years I had been away from cricket. Prior to National Service, I had played my first Test series against England in Australia and was then a non-smoker and a teetotaller, having not long moved to Sydney from a dairy farm. At that stage I was also early to bed. I can remember that on my first trip away with NSW I roomed with Norm O'Neill and he was terrified that I would wake up at 3.00 or 4.00am as we had to do on the farm. He had been delighted when he had to wake me at about 9.00am to get ready to go to the ground. I changed somewhat in National Service, and maybe Bill thought that with the influence of Les, who was a non-drinker as well as a non-smoker, I would revert to my old habits.

Les was a good middle-order batsman from Victoria, and we settled into the Waldorf Hotel in London. We tossed to see who got the double bed, which is pretty normal, and we actually unpacked our bags in those days. Les had played one Test before the tour. As it turned out, this was to be the only Test he ever played.

As most of my room-mates over the years will testify, I'm not one for spending a lot of time in the room, and even at this early stage I headed out of the room fairly quickly to become acclimatised in that big city. We had to attend a press conference on our arrival then had no more official duties on our first day, so a couple of us met in the foyer ready for our escapade in the big city of London, which was a hell of a lot different to Dungog. When you have team-mates like Dave Renneberg, Brian Taber, and Ian Chappell in his pre-captaincy days, you don't worry too much about catching too many buses to do the sightseeing. They had already noticed that the front bar was open, and a quick discussion convinced us that the best way to get over our jet lag was to stay awake and then go to bed at the local time when it got dark.

We had heard a lot about the English beer prior to our arrival so we were very pleased when the barman announced that they had plenty of cold Foster's in their fridges. I don't think they had the same understanding of the word 'plenty' as we did because they had to call for more supplies before we finished. By the time the local sleep time came around, I can assure you that nobody had any trouble sleeping. My room-mate Les Joslin didn't fare as well, however, as he had slept during the day and was awake reading all night. This didn't worry me one bit, especially that night. The next morning was our first practice session at Lord's, and this was to set the scene for the entire 1968 tour. The wickets were wet, so our practice session wasn't all that flash. I still wonder whether I made up my mind about English wickets that day, as I never fully came to grips with them.

During the first couple of weeks in England there were numerous official functions and many were black-tie luncheons and dinners. It didn't take my room-mate long to recognize my nocturnal tendencies. As soon as functions finished he was in bed with a book. If there wasn't a function, he was in bed before the sun set. He actually settled into a good sleep pattern though after his first few days, but when it came to the first match that he was to play in, sleep deserted him. If he was playing I could arrive back in the room long after he would normally be finished reading to find him wide awake. He said that as soon as he turned off the light he had visions of fast bowlers charging towards him and he couldn't go to sleep. My suggestion to him was that he should get himself down to the bar with us and have a couple of beers or a gin and tonic or something that might help with his sleeping problem. Les refused all suggestions and unfortunately he didn't have a great tour. His cricket at first-class level, in fact, didn't last very long after that tour and he disappeared off the scene.

I ran into Les about 15 years later when I was doing a beer promotion in a pub in Geelong and I was amazed to see that my ex-roomy had a large glass of beer in one hand and a cigarette in the other. He explained that just as I had started while working for a cigarette company, he had done the same. He obviously wasn't drinking the first beer of his life either. By this time he agreed that he might have been better off if he had taken my advice all those years before.

I'm not suggesting that these habits are the best model to follow, not by a long shot, but if Les Joslin had joined us in the Waldorf bar, he might have felt a little more relaxed about his cricket. He certainly would have had more sleep, because even with the late hours I kept I think I had more sleeping time than he did. Anyway he was a delightful roomy. Not too many others in the team would have waited up for me to come home.

The tour was stacked with heaps of matches. We played all the counties as well as the five Test matches. There were no one-day matches at that stage, but as it turned out weatherwise, there might as well have been. The summer of 1968 turned out to be one of the wettest in England's history. Those who know about wet English summers say, 'The rain in Spain falls mainly in England'. That was the first of four tours I was lucky enough to make to England.

I also made two tours to New Zealand and one to Ceylon (now Sri Lanka), India and South Africa combined, as well as the West Indies—all with Australian cricket teams. I didn't end up having any more teetotallers as room-mates, but enjoyed the company of all who I had. In my day there weren't any curfews, but you had to make sure you carried your weight on the cricket field.

Terry Jenner was my room-mate during the West Indies tour of 1973. Ian Chappell captained this tour. In Kingston, the Red Stripe Brewery set up our own 'private brewery' on the balcony of our room. It became known as Club Nine, since this was our room number. After being there with this set-up for two weeks I had a whole new appreciation of the saying, 'It smells like a brewery'.

T.J. (Terry Jenner) played a few more Tests than Les Joslin, but he didn't quite fulfil all his ambitions on the cricket field. The one thing he wanted to do, yet didn't, was to win a Test for his country with the ball in his hands. He may well have contributed towards this to some degree and on one occasion in Adelaide he may have won a Test with his bat. He scored 74 against England. The one that got away from him was the fourth Test in Guyana against the West Indies. The wicket was starting to take a lot of spin towards the end of the Test.

The great commentator Alan McGilvray invited T.J. up to his

room. We used to knock Alan up sometimes after the bar had closed if we were still thirsty, as he would always have a spare bottle in his room. He had asked Terry in because he had noticed that the wicket was deteriorating and wanted to have a chat in private. On arrival in Alan's room, Terry was overawed because Keith Miller was there as well. Keith asked Terry what it felt like to be on the verge of winning a Test for your country. Both Keith and Alan offered suggestions as to the end he should bowl from and gave him plenty of drinks along with the advice they offered. By the time Terry left Alan's room he was on top of the world and dearly wanted to talk to someone about his ambitions. He claims it was too early to find me so he rang some mates in Australia and he didn't get a great deal of sleep that night with all the excitement he was feeling. He had a few warm-up overs in the nets the next morning and he was primed up ready to fire.

Ian Chappell was surprised with the end that Terry chose to bowl from, but went along with him and suggested that I should bowl the opening over to change him to the end of his preference. Well, history records the fact that I got two wickets in the second innings, and Jeff Hammond and Max Walker got rid of the rest. Poor T.J. did not bowl a ball.

As I mentioned, my first tour was nearly seven months long, as was the combined Ceylon, India and South African tour of 1969–70. Since then, tours have become somewhat shorter. My last tour to England in 1977 was just over four months. The beauty of touring with the Australian cricket team is that the accommodation is generally close to first class. An exception to this was the three months we spent in India in 1969, where we were often accommodated at the grounds and were not very comfortable at all.

England is my pick of the tours, mainly because it is a small country and the distances between match venues can easily be reached by bus. Bus travel is much more leisurely than plane.

There was often time to relax with a game of golf on the English tours, and Denham Golf Club just out of London became like a second home, we spent so much time there. It's just as well I have never taken my golf too seriously, though, as I'm sure it would have driven me mad with frustration. By the way, it's not true the only hundreds I scored in England were on that golf course.

To some degree, the best tours are the ones where the team plays well. However, the tour to South Africa in 1969–70, where we were beaten 4–0, was an exception. The hospitality we were shown there was second to none. To a certain degree a tour is as good as you make it and you often make your own fun. With 17 players on an English tour there are a variety of personalities so you always find some that want to do the things that you enjoy.

Sightseeing was never something I spent a lot of time doing on tour. I've never owned a camera, so don't expect to see lots of tourist photos in this book. Meeting people, however, is something which I have always enjoyed and is still a big part of my life. I have met royalty on a number of occasions and that remains a highlight for me. On my first tour when Princess Margaret approached me and asked me to sing her a few verses of 'The Wild West Show', I was a bit lost for words at first. However, it didn't take too long to work out that our number-one wicket-keeper, Barry Jarman, had a lot to do with her request. Fortunately I talked my way out of it.

Probably there were 'troublemakers' in all sides that I toured with. On one of my first trips away with NSW, Frank Misson told the fruit fly inspector at Adelaide Airport that I had a bag full of bananas and other fruit in my possession. I actually think the fruit fly man was disappointed when he didn't find any, but it made Frank's day and schooled me well for the future. In the end I think I found more trick shops than anyone else around the world so I guess I have a few apologies to make.

The late Les Truman was treasurer on my first tour of

England. He wasn't at all impressed when I tipped ink all over his immaculate white suit when we were all ready to leave for a royal function. All was forgiven, however, as it dried and disappeared. Ashley Mallett's dislike for snakes and spiders gave me plenty of fun. I can still see the cricket ball disappearing over the boundary fence in South Africa in 1969–70. Ashley threw it after I handed it to him with a rubber spider stuck to it with chewing gum.

There were not as many tours when I played, but we did enjoy them. I'm not sure if I was playing these days that I would look forward to the tours as I once did. The players of today are on the go every year and sometimes to more than one country. To me, in my time, touring was a great experience where I made lifelong friends. I saw a lot of cricket grounds, bars, golf courses and racecourses in different parts of the world but, as I said, sightseeing wasn't my go. When I went to China on a promotional tour I was happy to see the Great Wall from the bus. I didn't feel that I needed to get out and walk on it like all the others had to do. I said, 'Seen one wall up close, you've seen the lot'. Apart from that, it was a hot day, the bus was air-conditioned and we just happened to have an esky on board with a few cold ones inside.

I do feel lucky to have had the opportunity to do these things, however. Days like Royal Ascot in top hat and tails take some beating. There are many privileges when you are part of an Australian cricket team. People in all parts of the world go out of their way to make you feel welcome.

We also got to some theatre and cabaret shows. It was wonderful to meet the original Seekers in England. You tend to forget that people at the top in other sports and professions enjoy cricket and it is great to be able to meet these famous people from all walks of life while on cricket tours. One of our managers often remarked, 'Money couldn't buy it', and I guess he was right.

WALKERS, TALKERS,
SNORERS AND EARTHQUAKES

*"Man, you get killed tomorrow. See here, this is a piece of
Mike Gatting's nose where Malcolm Marshall hit him."*

Professional cricket is spreading these days, with more and
more countries playing in the Test and the one-day arenas. All
the cricket countries want to make more money so touring is
now a much bigger part of the game than it has ever been. We
tour for almost half the year overseas and even when we're in
Australia we are usually on the road.

Being able to cope with touring is a very important part of
the modern cricketer's make up. You simply have to be able to
handle it or you won't survive. There are, of course, great
things about touring. We get to experience a great mixture of
cultures and landscapes. I would probably never have gone to
South Africa, Zimbabwe and Sri Lanka if it hadn't been for

cricket. Most of the places we go to are fantastic and interesting. You also begin to truly appreciate how wonderful Australia is and how lucky we are in this country. Just go to Pakistan and India and see the poverty. You'll soon appreciate the comforts of home.

Basically my job is terrific. I get paid to travel the world and play cricket. It's a wonderful life that I couldn't have imagined for myself when I was growing up. The cricketers are very fortunate. We get treated like kings on tour overseas. People carry our bags and we're taken to all the tourist and recreation spots, whether it's a game of golf on a famous course or the Taj Mahal.

We get to see sporting events like Wimbledon and the F.A. Cup. In Zimbabwe we visited Victoria Falls, in England we met the Queen and in South Africa we went on an amazing safari. On the other hand we're away from home. That's definitely hard. Most people are ready to come back from holidays after a few weeks. We're gone for months at a time. You have to adjust and learn how to live this nomadic life. It's particularly tough on family who are left behind.

We are constantly out of our comfort zones in terms of food, weather and accommodation. Your health suffers. Quite often in India and Pakistan you can feel sick for most of the tour. Some of the players don't handle it and that's why they produce modest results away but good results at home. Sometimes the main problem is boredom. In Pakistan there's not really anywhere to go. We often sit in our hotel rooms quite bored. In India people mob you the moment you leave the hotels, and quite often the hotel room is the only safe option. In Sri Lanka security worries also mean solitary confinement in your room for much of the time.

Naturally you're forced to make your own fun. We play games, watch videos, sleep, read, and write our books in some cases. Some of the guys play cards and we'll occasionally visit the High Commission. There are also media commitments. I tend to sleep a lot when I'm in Pakistan. We have fines meetings where fines are handed out to guys for being late or wearing the wrong gear. There are silly fines for doing stupid things.

Stephen is a real Tommy Tourist and he'll be out in the streets or at the markets. I have to admit that in most countries I tend to stick to the hotel and the TV and that suits me, although I do participate in other activities as well.

In the end, though, touring is what you make it. If you go with a bad attitude then you'll never make it work for you. That's why many teams haven't gone well in Pakistan. They're beaten before they arrive. I try to be positive and look forward to a tour, and that helps me to cope well. A lot of people will knock the food in Pakistan, for example, but last time we were there it was great. There are also some very good Chinese and Italian restaurants providing choices, and I really enjoyed our last stay there. We played golf and visited various locals at their houses. We went to the Australian High Commission and went to a sailing club in Karachi. We were invited all over the place and were incredibly well looked after. Sometimes simple outings and activities like visiting the Australian High Commission, reading an Australian newspaper, or drinking a can of VB can really make a big difference.

Once I went to Pakistan and the hotel we were staying in wasn't finished. It would have been quite nice eventually but there was no room service at all, no air conditioning, no shower curtains, no TV. It was basically a box to sleep in. Another time in Patiala there was no linen, no breakfast, and large rats in the rooms. We were there for five days and it was before the first Test on that particular tour. Not the best preparation but we survived. You do get exposed to remarkable contrasts. We went to absolutely luxurious five-star hotels in Sun City in South Africa. In England and South Africa we stay in great places, and some of the Taj Hotels in India are extremely beautiful.

I like travelling to South Africa the most, and Cape Town in particular. The beaches, the golf and the safaris are fantastic. There's a lot to do. It's very similar to Australia in lifestyle and the food is excellent which helps you stay healthy. Staying well and feeling good within yourself are the two most difficult but most important tasks on tour.

The subject of room-mates has been written about in numerous cricket books and mostly in the funny-stories sections. Actually we mostly don't room with anyone anymore. For all Test matches we're in separate rooms and in Australia it's single rooms all the way, but when we're overseas the host country pays for the accommodation so it's only single rooms for Test matches. As it has often been said, rooming with another player can be interesting. Blokes snore and smoke and play their music. Still, most of them are pretty good and they'll give and take a fair bit.

I've never roomed with Stephen. The manager and captain assign the room-mates and perhaps they think that because we shared for 17 years growing up we've done our time with each other. I agree, enough is enough. (Only joking!)

I'm actually very happy with my own company and don't need to be socialising all the time on tour. Other guys really need people around them constantly. Craig McDermott as a room-mate was always there. You'd go into the bathroom and he'd be right there behind you talking away. He had faxes coming in every day. It was amazing.

I quite often room with Warnie. The phone never stops ringing for him. It's always fans. You may as well be rooming with Bono. He sometimes smokes as well, and I don't. They usually try to put the smokers, like Shane, Darren Lehmann, Tim May, Boonie, together. They were together most of the time but it doesn't always work out that way. The thing is, we're all good mates and nobody is perfect—least of all me, so I'm told by the others. Snoring and talking are my two downfalls. They also say I hog the bathroom, but I just can't see it.

There are the snorers. Michael Bevan is a very light sleeper and he can't room with anyone who snores. I remember he roomed with Mark Taylor in a Shield match last year and I think Mark woke up in the morning and found Michael curled up on the bathroom floor. Tim May and Darren Lehmann are in the grand final for the loudest snore. Stephen roomed with Tim a lot. I just take ear plugs with me these days and that can take care of most of the noise.

Then there are the talkers. Justin Langer talks all night, and when I roomed with him in the West Indies, he was talking in his sleep with a West Indian accent. 'How ya goin', Man? Cool Man.' I was awake most of the night, but he can't remember it at all. Jason Gillespie talks all night in what sounds like a foreign language.

Some guys walk in their sleep. I think it was Heals who was sharing with Craig McDermott when Craig thought there were kangaroos in the room. He was hiding behind the curtain from them in his sleep. I shared with him in Pakistan once when there was an earth tremor at 6.00am. The paintings were swaying on the walls and lamps were falling over. Craig jumped up in his sleep and said, 'Junior, stop jumping on my bed'. I said, 'Craig, don't worry about me jumping on your bed, it's a bloody earthquake'.

So there are a few guys who are tough to room with. It's something that's been overlooked a bit in the past. If you don't sleep well it's hard to perform the next day. We have said this constantly to administrators over the years and they've said, 'Oh, they'll be right'. But quite often it can be a real problem. I think it's very important that we have single rooms so we can relax and sleep well. It always amazed me that the scorer, the physio, the manager and other non-players would have single rooms but not the players. I could never figure it out. These days, however, the ACB has come to the party and it is no longer a problem in Australia.

Also our partners are now pretty well free to go where they

want. The days of banning them from the team hotel are more or less over. We do have to pay for them of course, although the ACB brought the girls over towards the end of the 1999 West Indies tour for a holiday. We never take them to Pakistan or India but they do come to England and New Zealand. Most of them come over. They are actually encouraged to be there a bit more these days. People bring their young children too. There's so much more cricket now that if they didn't come we'd never see them at all. At the start of a tour, though, the partners and kids usually won't stay with us because the team needs to bond and prepare.

As the tours progress, the girls usually join us and stay with us for most of the time. In England they might rent a house and stay together. They'll also come and watch us at county games and stay with friends in the various places. We do want to have our partners with us but it can be awkward if we've played all day and feel tired, and they've been watching all day and want to go out to a restaurant. We'll often want to relax and focus on being a team. There has to be give and take on both sides.

Touring can be a very solitary life. You have your particular mates in the team that you talk to about things, including matters that are personal or private. That helps, and you do look out for each other, but the people you're really close to just aren't there much of the time. The bottom line is you're pretty well by yourself. I cope quite well with this.

We spend a lot of time on tour travelling. In England we travel by bus from county to county and elsewhere we fly. In Australia we travel economy, except to Perth, and travelling overseas we fly business class, then economy within the actual countries. We spend hours and hours in airports. Everywhere we go we are met by a liaison officer who looks after us.

In India and Pakistan we never see our bags. You pack it and put it outside your room and it arrives at the next hotel. We are extremely well looked after. In Australia we lug our own bags while the visiting teams are looked after, with bags being carried and all that goes with it. In that sense, it is better for us overseas, but I'm not complaining. They assume you can fend for yourself in your own country, which is fair enough.

The West Indies is a really interesting place to tour. Each island has a distinctly different culture, of course. Barbados is very relaxed and a great place to be, with its fantastic beaches and restaurants. On the other hand in Kingston, Jamaica, we can't leave the hotel by ourselves because it's a bit rough. We're warned about the dangers. Even at the ground, part of the crowd is fenced off. You can smell the marijuana. In Kingston they love to see the ball fly around the head. The aggressive side of the game really appeals to them.

In 1991 we were there before a game inspecting the pitch and the groundsman was there with us. We were saying, 'Gee this looks like a bouncy, fast pitch', and the groundsman said, 'Man, you get killed tomorrow. See here, this is a piece of Mike Gatting's nose where Malcolm Marshall hit him.' He went on, 'That be you tomorrow, Man'. I thought that was pretty rough.

Then you go to Antigua and it's just a great party all day, with live music and a juke-box blaring. They have these two guys in the crowd called Mayfair and Gravy. They're usually dressed up as women, sometimes in nurses' uniforms. They wear these immense boxing gloves and have a fight on the ground in front of the crowd. One day when they were dressed up in the nurses' outfits I was going in to bat in a Test match and one of them followed me onto the ground. He ran up to me and took out this big stethoscope and placed it on my chest as if testing my heartbeat. It was unbelievable. It put me off my game. I got out first ball!

Can you imagine someone at Lord's running out with you from the crowd dressed in drag? It's just so different and relaxed. A lot of fun actually. The hotels we stay in are on the beach and if it wasn't for the cricket it would be a great holiday.

CHAPTER FIVE

DREAM TEAMS

MOSTLY LOCAL HEROES

*'I would rate Sir Garfield Sobers as the best batsman
I have ever seen.'*

I think choosing dream teams is something that you are better off doing in your sleep than when you are awake because you'll always forget someone or make cases for plenty of others that could go into the 12.

I'll begin with my era, and I hasten to apologise to those who do not make it, but I think this side would beat most others you care to put it against. Therefore, this is a team of players chosen from those I have played with and against. I will list my team in my preferred batting order. Here goes.

Geoff Boycott, Gordon Greenidge, Ian Chappell, Viv Richards, Garfield Sobers, Greg Chappell, Graeme Pollock, Alan Knott, Richard Hadlee, Dennis Lillee, Derek Underwood. I would have Jeff Thomson carrying the drinks.

I'm sure that the idea of choosing dream teams was only mooted with the aim of causing an argument. I know that I could even be persuaded that about 20 other guys would be unlucky not to make this team. I know that Bill Lawry and Bob Simpson were a very successful opening pair for Australia for a long time, and Desmond Haynes has great qualifications, as does Sunil Gavaskar and a number of others. However, you can only send out two to open the innings.

Boycott might not be high on the list of many people to open an innings because he wasn't a quick scorer, but he was a very good player just the same. Of course I couldn't have Boycott and Lawry opening an innings together, as this would go against my grain and I wouldn't want to totally demoralize every bowler they opposed together. Just imagine this combination together—I don't think there would be any bowlers left. It would be just like bowling at a brick wall, with neither prepared to take any chances whatsoever. I have to pick a team which would give the opposition bowlers some chance to make it entertaining. I'm sure that both these players would aim to have his captain win the toss and allow them to go on batting right throughout the entire Test match. Five days would not daunt either of them, nor would the fact that nobody else would get a bat. I've selected Boycott, however, because he has a great record, and he is the only Stonewall Jackson in my team, if I were to need one.

The only way Gordon Greenidge knows how to play is to attack and punish the bowler from the very first ball he faces, so he would be a very good foil with the opening mate I've settled on. It will also ensure that the scoreboard attendant stays awake. Ian Chappell is capable of playing both attack and defence if Boycott should happen to go early. I'm not suggesting that he's anywhere near the snail's pace of Boycott, but he has proven himself under all conditions and he would make an excellent captain of my team.

I think just the sight of Viv Richards walking to the wicket would be enough to put most bowlers off. Many people have told me that Viv is arrogant, possibly because of his confident stroll to the wicket, but I've always found him to be a delightful fellow. It's funny how people have preconceived ideas about a person's nature without even meeting him or her. Bowlers would need to have plenty of confidence when bowling to Viv because it is possible they might start to lose it very quickly. Viv likes to set bowlers back on their heels from the first ball he faces. If he can (and he often does) whack it to the boundary, then that sets the style for the rest of his innings. From then on bowlers just need good luck. Bradman could well have played far more noteworthy innings than Viv, but I don't think he could have been more convincing than either Viv, or the number five batsman I have named.

I would rate Sir Garfield Sobers as the best batsman I have ever seen. I could not have a dream team without including him. As well as batting, Garfield Sobers had the ability to bowl fast as well as spin the ball in both orthodox and unorthodox methods, and to top it off, he could field brilliantly in all positions. I could say that he would be the perfect cricketer. With his elegant style, I would expect Greg Chappell to add another century batting at number six.

I listed Graeme Pollock as coming in at number seven, only because I couldn't find a spot for him any higher in the batting order. I also think he would be the best partner for the remaining batsmen. I rate Graeme as the best 'farmer' of the strike that I ever came across. His footwork may not have been equal to the batsmen ahead of him, but Graeme was, none the less, very effective. Because of South Africa's isolation from international cricket we didn't get to see nearly enough of this wonderful player in his younger days.

I have selected Alan Knott to bat at number eight because he was a dogged batsman who could hold his wicket intact and he would be the ideal person to bat with Pollock. Of course Alan Knott is in the side as the wicket-keeper. He had amazing ability to handle all bowlers and I have to give him the nod. Richard Hadlee is another bowler, who was very handy with the bat in his day. He carried the New Zealand bowling attack single handedly and was an excellent performer on all types of wickets.

Coming in at number ten, Dennis Lillee may not score a lot of runs but will most certainly make someone work for his wicket. I rate Dennis as the king of fast bowlers. He just doesn't know how to give in. Dennis still gives one hundred percent, regardless of the pitch or the state of the match—a truly great fast bowler.

The number eleven position has to be filled by a spin bowler to assist Sobers. In my opinion, the best man for that job would be Derek Underwood. Derek wouldn't score too many runs but he shouldn't have to, with the batting line-up I've selected. Derek had a wonderful variety of deliveries on all wickets, and for this reason, he has earned my vote.

I have given Jeff Thomson the job of carrying the drinks. I think he would be carrying them for a long time, waiting for any of the team-mates I've selected to break down. I feel that Thommo was the fastest bowler I ever came across, and I doubt that anyone will ever bowl faster.

I know that there will be a lot of arguments to follow my selections. Allan Border has been omitted for a start, but there just aren't enough places for all the players I could include. However, I can tell you that this team would win more games than it would lose and, personally, I would hate to be bowling against it. Anyone who played this team would want to love fielding too because they would spend a great deal of their time chasing leather.

Choosing a team from available players over the last century is even more provocative. In choosing a team from this scope of players, I must say that I am mostly going by what I have heard and read in record books. I will list this team in batting order as well.

My team is: Bill Ponsford, who was a prolific scorer, opening with Arthur Morris, who I have some bias towards because he spent part of his childhood in Dungog. The great man, and captain of the team, Donald Bradman, would be number three. Since he was the world's greatest ever player, he deserves to be the skipper. Number four would be Neil Harvey, the fantastic left-handed master strokes maker. Viv Richards and Garfield Sobers make this team as well, as numbers five and six.

At number seven I will then add Keith Miller, another superb all rounder who was capable of doing anything with either the bat or the ball. I have selected Don Tallon as the wicket-keeper and number eight in this team, as he was also a handy batsman. Shane Warne comes in at number nine because he is the best spinner I have seen.

The number ten position would go to Clarrie Grimmett. It has been said that he just went giddy taking wickets. He must have been an incredible spinner. Dennis Lillee would make this team as well, at number eleven. Lillee and Miller, supported by Sobers, would be a fantastic early bowling attack, and then to have these fellows backed up by Warne and Grimmett would do me. I don't think it would be fair to name a twelfth man in this side. I've got to admit that my team is overloaded with Australians, but I don't apologize for that. I will tell you that from this team I have only seen Lillee, Sobers, Richards, Warne and Harvey play. I have relied on history books to do the rest.

My co-author would know far more about the dream team of the modern day, because he has played with or against all of them. However, I will have a go at selecting a team from this current era of players. I would begin with Michael Slater opening the innings. If he fires, then the team will automatically be in a winning position. For Michael's opening partner, I would choose Gary Kirsten from South Africa. He is a good solid opener.

In the number three position, I would have Sachin Tendulkar from India. Tendulkar is a prolific run scorer who seems to keep on improving every year. Brian Lara would come in at number four. He has been disappointing at times, but he still holds many records so I think these warrant his inclusion by me.

The number five position would go to Mark Waugh, because I would want to watch him in any side, and I would also select his twin brother, Steve, at number six. Steve has been very successful in this position for a long time. Ian Healy would be given the number seven spot, because he revels in situations when the top order fails. I think Ian is a top wicket-keeper/batsman, and his value in this current team has been underestimated. His keeping to Shane Warne alone has been outstanding, but he keeps well to all bowlers.

Wasim Akram impresses me at number eight because he tries his heart out all day, and he has the ability to swing old balls an incredible amount. Wasim also bats better than most fast bowlers do. At number nine I would include Shane Warne, followed by Allan Donald at number ten. Donald has proven himself as a top line bowler day in and day out over a number of years. I would have to have Glenn McGrath batting at number eleven. He is trying hard to improve his batting, and he has succeeded in lifting this aspect of his game, but I still don't think he is ready to move up any higher in my team. Besides that, Glenn has obviously been included for his fantastic bowling. He doesn't waste any deliveries and is still continuing to improve year by year.

The way Lance Klusener bowled and batted in the most recent World Cup he deserves his place as a drinks waiter. I haven't seen a more punishing hitter for a long time.

It will be interesting to compare Mark's team with mine, but I will back this selection to win, or at least have any opposition flat-out trying to beat them. From this current selection, I would give the captaincy job to Steve Waugh. Of course I would like an Aussie to lead the team. In all three teams combined, I have selected 18 Australians out of 33, but I think they deserve their inclusion.

If I was to pick my teams again, I might even add more Australians because I like the way we play our cricket in this country. I don't believe in computer cricket, but I don't think the computer would throw in names that were vastly different to those I've selected. Anyhow, I'm prepared to have a small wager on any of my three teams up against anybody else's, and I wish them good luck.

ENTERTAIN ME!

'Sachin Tendulkar is, I believe, the best current player in the world. He's my number four. He has the most refined technique and scores runs at will—especially against us . . .'

Choosing dream teams has become something of a national pastime whatever the code or sport. It is always a controversial thing to do but it is also an irresistible exercise when you're really interested in a particular game and if you know something about the history of a game.

The first dream team I'll select is my team from the current players around the world—my contemporaries. I base most of my selections for all three dream teams in this chapter around match-winning and aggressive players. I have never liked defensive players. The game is not just there for winning, it should also be entertaining. That's why, as you'll see, for the most part

85

I've chosen players who are exciting to watch. They are the players who tend to win matches from aggressive play.

For the team from my era I've chosen Sanath Teran Jayasuriya as the opening batsman. He is a dynamic sort of player and scores very quickly. I love watching him play. He's improved a hundred percent over the last two years and he's definitely who I want as my opening batsman.

Another opener I'd select is Mark Taylor. His record is outstanding and has been outstanding over a long period of time—more than a hundred Tests—and he averages in the mid-40s. He's scored 19 Test centuries over the years. I'd put him in as the steady opening influence. Both Saeed Anwar and Michael Slater are, however, also outstanding players and could equally slot in here.

Number three is Brian Lara from the West Indies. He's simply a great player who can win matches single-handedly. One of the top three in the world along with Stephen and Sachin Tendulkar, he averages over 50 and has the world record highest score in Test and first-class cricket.

Sachin Tendulkar is, I believe, the best current player in the world. He's my number four. He has the most refined technique and scores runs at will—especially against us (the current Australian side). I'd certainly want him playing for us rather than against us, if I had a choice.

At number five I'd select my brother Stephen. Better put him in. His record speaks for itself, particularly over the last few years. He's a very consistent, tough player. He plays very well under pressure and has adapted his game to suit his strengths. He averages over 50 in Test cricket.

I hate to admit this, but at number six I've sort of chosen myself. Is that too bigheaded? I'd really want to be in this team. I've actually bracketed myself for this spot with Aravinda de Silva from Sri Lanka and Graham Thorpe from England. So there's three of us battling it out at number six.

That's stretching the rules of selection a bit, I know.

The wicket-keeper at number seven has to be Ian Healy. He has taken the most catches ever. He's a great competitor, and it's not only his wicket-keeping, he also bats very well. The way he's kept to the spinners over the years—especially Shane Warne—has been remarkable. That's a very tough thing to do. He is by far and away the best wicket-keeper in the world.

Wasim Akram from Pakistan at number eight is a must for any dream team. He's a match-winning bowler with unlimited ability. He bowls fast and can swing the ball. He can bowl yorkers. He's a real wicket-taker and can turn a match around with ball and bat.

Shane Warne is the best spinner in the world. He has taken the most wickets of any spin bowler in the history of the game. So that speaks for itself. He's number nine.

I'd choose Curtly Ambrose from the West Indies at number ten. He also has a great record. He doesn't bowl any bad balls. He's the complete champion.

I'd better put Glenn McGrath in at number eleven or he'll get dirty. Seriously though, he's very similar to Curtly. He bowls fast and never gives anything away. They're both very strong, tough competitors.

My number twelve is Allan Donald. You can really bracket Ambrose, McGrath and Donald together as three of the top four bowlers in the world. The fourth is, of course, Akram.

My captain is Mark Taylor. He has the best track record in this group and is the obvious one to lead the team.

Now I'll list my dream team from Doug's era. I have actually played with and against some of these players, although others I've only read and heard about or watched.

My opening batsman would be Barry Richards from South Africa. I didn't see him play a lot and he didn't play much Test cricket but almost everyone you speak to rates him as one of the best players ever in the world. He averaged over 70 in Test cricket and over 50 in first-class cricket. It doesn't get much better than that and he would be my first opener in this team. The other opener would be Sunil Gavaskar from India. He averages over 50 and has a tremendous record.

At number three I'd select Greg Chappell. He has always been one of my very favourite players. He has a tremendous record and is a very attacking player, although he's also extremely graceful and classy with the bat. I'd always be happy to pay to watch him play.

Viv Richards at number four is my all-time favourite player, and always has been. He's the best player I've ever seen and I'd make him captain of this team. From when I started watching cricket, he has been the player I always took the greatest interest in. He has all the shots and he hits the ball extremely hard. I like the arrogant look about him. I have been very fortunate to play against Viv quite a lot and got him out in a Test match in Barbados in 1991. He's so memorable the way he chews gum and struts around. He has an aura around him and he stares at you without flinching. His presence at the crease almost scares you even though he's only batting.

Number five is Douggie. He's also one of my all-time favourites. He's got a great record. His average is about 48 in Test cricket. I like his casual approach and appearance but he's also an attacking player which is very appealing to me. I'll never forget the six he hit in Perth off the last ball of the day against Bob Willis to reach his hundred—what a great hook shot.

Garfield Sobers must be at number six. A great all-rounder who could bat, bowl and field brilliantly. The complete cricketer.

The wicket-keeper is Rod Marsh. The second best after Healy from what I've seen. So he's in at number seven.

Fast-bowling all-rounder Malcolm Marshall is eight. One of the best I've ever faced and watched bowl. He bowls fast, swings the ball—he can do anything. That combination is deadly. All the guys you speak to reckon he's one of the hardest to face with those fast swinging deliveries.

For my spinner it was a toss-up between Abdul Qadir or Derek Underwood. In the end I've gone for Underwood—a left-arm spinner. A bit of a dull bowler, but what a record!

They called Michael Holding from the West Indies 'Whispering Death' because he used to be so graceful as he ran to the crease and very light on his feet. Then the ball would fly hard and fast out of his hand. Very fast and top class. He's number ten.

Dennis Lillee, the Australian legend and probably our best ever fast bowler, is a must for the team at number eleven. My twelfth man is Kapil Dev, Richard Hadlee or Ian Botham. I can't decide. They're all great cricketers. I'll choose Ian Botham if pressed.

To select my best team from the whole century was very, very difficult, although a fascinating exercise at the turn of the new millennium. I've crossed players out and put them in and then crossed them out again. So, here goes.

I've gone for Gavaskar and Tendulkar, both from India, to open the batting. I can't fit Tendulkar in at three or four so I've put him in as an opener and believe he could play there just as well.

Number three is obviously Don Bradman with his extraordinary average of 99.94. He has to be there and this was the only really easy selection for me.

At number four I've gone for Australia's greatest-ever run scorer and that's Allan Border. He played when the team was pretty ordinary at one stage and played consistently well under pressure. He made an incredible effort, played an extraordinary number of games, and, as the highest run scorer we've ever produced, he deserves a place.

At number five I've chosen Viv Richards for all the reasons I gave above. Garfield Sobers at my number six was a great all-rounder. He could do anything with the ball, and his record speaks for itself. He was a king with the bat, averaging 50, and he could also catch. For me he was another obvious choice.

A devastating bowler, Wasim Akram is number seven. Being a left-hander too, I guess that provides a bit of variety. Ian Healy is my wicket-keeper again for all the reasons I've already stated, and I believe Shane Warne is the best spinner we've ever seen, so he's in at number nine.

Malcolm Marshall makes it again at number ten and Dennis Lillee at eleven. My twelfth man is Ian Botham. Then Bradman is captain with Viv Richards as his vice captain. That's it. Please don't write to me, it was hard enough getting this far.

A SUMMARY OF OUR DREAM TEAMS

Doug's Dream Team From His Own Era

1. Geoff Boycott
2. Gordon Greenidge
3. Ian Chappell (c)
4. Viv Richards
5. Garfield Sobers
6. Greg Chappell
7. Graeme Pollock
8. Alan Knott
9. Richard Hadlee
10. Dennis Lillee
11. Derek Underwood
12. Jeff Thomson

Mark's Dream Team From Doug's Era

1. Barry Richards
2. Sunil Gavaskar
3. Greg Chappell
4. Viv Richards (c)
5. Doug Walters
6. Garfield Sobers
7. Rod Marsh
8. Malcolm Marshall
9. Derek Underwood
10. Michael Holding
11. Dennis Lillee
12. Ian Botham

Doug's Dream Team From Current Players

1. Michael Slater
2. Gary Kirsten
3. Sachin Tendulkar
4. Brian Lara
5. Mark Waugh
6. Stephen Waugh (c)
7. Ian Healy
8. Wasim Akram
9. Shane Warne
10. Allan Donald
11. Glenn McGrath
12. Lance Klusener

Mark's Dream Team From Current Players

1. Sanath Teran Jayasuriya
2. Mark Taylor (c)
3. Brian Lara
4. Sachin Tendulkar
5. Stephen Waugh
6. Aavinda de Silva
   Graham Thorpe
   Mark Waugh
7. Ian Healy
8. Wasim Akram
9. Shane Warne
10. Curtly Ambrose
11. Glenn McGrath
12. Allan Donald

Doug's Dream Team From The Century	Mark's Dream Team From The Century
1. Bill Ponsford	1. Sunil Gavaskar
2. Arthur Morris	2. Sachin Tendulkar
3. Donald Bradman (c)	3. Donald Bradman (c)
4. Neil Harvey	4. Allan Border
5. Viv Richards	5. Viv Richards
6. Garfield Sobers	6. Garfield Sobers
7. Keith Miller	7. Wasim Akram
8. Don Tallon	8. Ian Healy
9. Shane Warne	9. Shane Warne
10. Clarrie Grimmett	10. Malcolm Marshall
11. Dennis Lillee	11. Dennis Lillee
12. No selection	12. Ian Botham

CHAPTER SIX

DOUG ON MARK
AND
MARK ON DOUG

WITH TIME ON HIS SIDE

'I am particularly interested in the fact that Mark seems to have so much extra time to play his shots.'

The first time I sighted Mark Waugh was at the Bankstown Indoor Cricket Centre. I watched him backhand a ball off the nets several times, and he hit the stumps almost every time whilst his back was still turned. Just about everyone knows Mark Waugh today, but at that stage it was different, and I asked the person next to me who he was. This fellow gave me Mark's name, and then added, 'Just watch him bat and bowl. He's pretty good, and he's got a twin brother out there who is also fairly handy.' I often reflect on those words 'pretty good' and 'fairly handy' and wonder what adjectives that fellow uses to describe the Waugh twins now.

I left the Centre that day with a lasting impression of some extraordinary talent. The person who had been sitting beside me at the match had also told me the Waughs were talented at soccer, tennis, golf and squash. He was right, it seems there is nothing these boys can't do. I had an interest in indoor cricket at the time and could see that Mark was special, something I also observed later when I saw both boys playing in representative indoor cricket teams all around Australia.

I happened to mention to someone else one day, 'I hope they're not just playing indoor cricket!' 'No,' I was told. 'They play outdoor cricket as well.' I was keen to see if Mark and Steve's outdoor game was as good as the indoor matches I had seen and, sure enough, it wasn't too long before they were both in the NSW Shield side.

Tooheys were the NSW cricket sponsors in those days and they also sponsored a Country Cup competition. The country competition involved a dozen or so matches that were played in neighbouring towns and cities throughout NSW. One town played against its neighbouring town, and each year the venues for the match were alternated so that the local cricket associations could benefit. Tooheys took six players who had either played at state level or were currently playing for NSW, and three played in each team.

The Waugh twins were soon invited to play in these matches and they were immediately successful because of their impressive cricket ability, which caused a great deal of interest in the country towns. In those days Mark bowled with deceptive pace, and he also belted the opposition bowlers to all parts of the grounds and out of them as well. I was astounded that Mark appeared to do this with the greatest of ease, and I knew immediately that I was watching something special. Mark was a very successful fast–medium bowler until back problems hindered this ability. Not to be daunted, however, the versatile Mark worked on bowling off-spin and he is now achieving equal success with these.

Although these bowling feats were impressive, Mark's batting and fielding abilities were also exceptional. I am particularly interested in the fact that Mark seems to have so much extra time to play his shots. His agility on the field gives me the same impression when he takes catches with so much ease. I had seen this amazing ability before in great players like Garfield Sobers, Norman O'Neill, Viv Richards, Graeme Pollock and Greg Chappell, and I wondered how Mark would handle this incredible talent which he possessed.

The record books now answer this question, as Mark has gone on to use his outstanding ability very well. I feel that there have been times when Mark has actually got himself out because of the extra time he appears to have on his side. He seems to manufacture shots that other players wouldn't even attempt. It might only be a fraction of a second, but the way Mark coordinates his movements with the time available is amazing. Although, as I mentioned, this could be the reason why Mark has got out on occasion, he has also scored hundreds of runs because of it.

Frequently people tell me that they would prefer to see Mark Waugh score 10 runs than watch most other batsmen go on to score a century. I have to say that I agree with these people one hundred percent. Mark has now combined careful placement with his elegant batting style making him a joy to watch. His placement wasn't always as immaculate as it is now, and this could have led to some dismissals earlier on in his career. Some time back Mark appeared to smash balls consistently enough, but unfortunately they were often straight to fieldsmen and this cost him plenty of runs.

Another outstanding ability which Mark possesses is his versatility in adjusting from Test cricket, where he bats at number four, to one-day cricket where he is required to open the innings. This change is far from easy. You have to think differently to make this change, as well as having to adjust your batting to cope with a swinging new ball. Mark does this with great success, even ridiculous ease. To watch Mark Waugh score a century is enough to make a lifelong convert of any person who has not previously watched and loved cricket. I have been privileged to see a number of these centuries and the good thing is that I know I am going to enjoy many more.

There is also talk of a number of fielders around the world being rated as the best at the moment, but I would certainly rank Mark amongst them. I say this because again his versatility shows on the field as he demonstrates well above-average ability in all positions. I have seen Mark take extremely difficult catches and make them look simple.

During the Country Cup matches Mark and I shared many beers and yarns. We have often had a bet on the same horses. However, he follows the trots more than I do. Perhaps that's because the hours of the trotting meetings fit in better with the time he is on the cricket field. I used to try to follow the trots as well, and sometimes the dogs too, but it got extremely complicated and time consuming. When it became more nerve-racking than playing cricket, I thought I should stick to the gallops. However I still have an interest in a few of Mark's runners from time to time. Unfortunately, to date, this interest has taken on the complexion of a fishing story, with Mark saying things like, 'you should have bet on him last week . . .'

I wasn't sure until now whether Mark has any ambition to captain a team, but he has been given the vice-captaincy role a couple of times. I suspect that Mark might be just as happy without that extra responsibility, and sometimes this is a bonus so you can concentrate on your own game. However, since Mark's elder brother (by some minutes) is in charge these days, he might get the chance to have a little say in the directing of matches.

Mark gives me the impression that he just loves playing cricket. I'm sure that millions of other people are in agreement with me when I say I hope that enjoyment and desire to play stay with him for many years to come.

During a photo session for this book, Mark and I were both asked to wear an Australian cap and blazer. I took my first blazer out of the wardrobe and dutifully donned it to have some photos taken with Mark. I must say he astounded me yet again when he looked at my blazer pocket and baggy green cap and read 1965–66. Mark then said loudly, '1965, that was the year I was born'. Well Mark may be a lot younger than I am, but I feel that I know him well and can call him a friend. Although I have not seen very much of Mark socially since the Country Cup days, our paths sometimes cross on other occasions and I think that the nods we exchange say a great deal about the admiration we have for each other. I wish Mark every ounce of success for the future.

Perhaps we may not find out about Mark's potential as an Australian captain, but he has proven many times that he is a match-winner. In my opinion there is no better model today for any aspiring young cricketer.

YOU CAN TAKE THE BOY OUT
OF DUNGOG ...

*'I was pretty smart. I would sit on one beer while
Doug had about five.'*

When I first started playing cricket Greg Chappell and Doug
Walters were the two batsmen I admired the most in the
Australian cricket team. I think I was particularly drawn to
Doug because of his seemingly relaxed game and his casual,
down-to-earth attitude. I still like his very open, easy-going
nature.

Back then when I first became aware of him, nothing seemed
to worry him. He never appeared to become upset. I wanted to
imitate the way he batted, scoring very quickly and not letting
anything rattle him. To me he was a completely natural player,
and I aspired to be the same. Everything he did, whether it was
chipping in with a vital wicket, making a brilliant stop in the

covers or cracking a square cut, he always looked in control and executed with a minimum of fuss.

The most memorable shot for me that Doug played was when he hit that six in Perth against England to reach his century. It was literally the last ball of the day and he hooked a towering six to get there. I will never forget that day. I was only nine but even then I loved to watch him play.

Bob Willis was the bowler that day—a quality pace bowler, but Douggie dispatched him like a medium pacer. Doug's record against the great West Indies was outstanding, and a sure sign he could really bat.

I first met Doug at a World Series coaching clinic at Cranbrook School. I was being coached and he was instructing. I got his autograph because he was one of my favourite players. It was a prized autograph and I notice that even today when I've been involved in the odd coaching clinic with Doug, his autograph is as popular as ever.

When I first played for NSW we had a competition called the Tooheys Cup. Two local country teams would play each other—for example, Newcastle would play Gosford—and each team would include three state players. It was an exhibition match but it would give the locals a chance to rub shoulders with the best. I was one of those state players and Doug was working for Tooheys. He was always at the games and would play, even though he was a bit older than us. We'd play about six games a year all over the state. Crowds would be huge in the country towns with 5,000 people regularly turning up to watch. Doug was a hit with everyone.

We saw each other at all those games in Dubbo, Albury, Wagga, Port Macquarie, Coffs Harbour, Taree—everywhere. I'd always mix with Doug on those trips. He'd tell cricket stories in the bar until all hours, and obviously our horseracing interest also drew us together. We'd always go down to the TAB together on days off. It was a ritual for Doug to have at least ten bets for the day. He would have a pocket full of tickets, mostly trifectas, quinellas and doubles.

The tours usually lasted over three or four days so on the first day Doug would go to all the pubs in town that had Tooheys on tap and he'd stay for an hour talking to the locals and handing out tickets to the game. He'd have a drink or two. It was a learning curve for me because I was the new kid on the block. I was there to promote cricket and promote Tooheys.

I was pretty smart. I would sit on one beer while Doug had about five. We'd talk about cricket and the races. He was a legend and everyone wanted to talk to him, get an autograph or shake his hand. I was only just coming onto the scene and no one really knew who I was at all. Doug was the absolute centre of attention. They loved him, and he was completely natural and generous towards everyone. I would just sit there and take everything in.

The next day we'd do a coaching clinic, and once again he'd be completely helpful and patient with all the kids. He's very good at that sort of thing and really helps them out. Then after that we'd do the pubs again and *then* play cricket. I don't know how we fronted, but we did, and Doug never seemed the worse for wear. He was always the last to leave the bar, and his behaviour in the bar wouldn't alter from the time he arrived at the bar at 7.00pm until the time he left at midnight. He'd front up the next day apparently completely well. I don't know how he does it.

The main thing I want to stress about Douggie is that he's still exactly the same bloke. He's absolutely never changed. He's always casual—not uncaring but just relaxed and at ease with himself. I swear he still wears the same clothes—the grey trousers and the polo shirt handed out for Tooheys Cup games all those years ago. The impressive thing is that he still fits into them. I'm not so sure I'd still fit into mine.

Doug took a supporters tour to England in 1998 and apparently they couldn't get him out of Ladbrokes (England's version of the TAB). They reckon the tour party never saw him because he was always in the bar having a bet and a drink. Only Doug could confirm or deny this. I still see him around quite a bit, but he doesn't push forward or often come up to you on tour to say hello. He just does his own thing and is very self-contained. I like that style. He doesn't take advantage of his cricketing record and doesn't float around social circles. It's very refreshing to find someone like this. I'm sure he'd still know and keep in touch with all the blokes from Dungog.

Doug's dry and simple sense of humour has made him a legend on the guest-speaking circuit. So popular is he, that I think he's been to almost every town in Australia. The only problem is that he's constantly having to learn new stories because he's always invited back.

Doug is a great role model for young cricketers. I have tried to incorporate a lot of his game into mine over the years. I have tried to adopt his unflappable temperament and his natural flowing batting style. Despite these apparently relaxed qualities, he has remained as competitive as anybody who has donned the baggy green.

Hopefully there will always be some Douggie Walters characters representing Australia because I believe he represents many of our best qualities. There's always a lot of joking about him being a larrikin and liking a drink or two, but in fact there's so much more than meets the eye. I think you just have to look at the considered way he coaches the younger players to appreciate his knowledge, patience and the care that he's prepared to hand on to others.

CHAPTER SEVEN

OUR LOVE OF PUNTING

THE IMPOSSIBLE DREAM

*'This was not a great start to my gambling career,
and our next meal allowance payment was not due
for another fortnight.'*

My introduction to gambling started on my first tour of England in 1968. Prior to this I was like millions of other Australians—putting the odd dollar on the Melbourne Cup and that was about the extent of my interest. My first couple of attempts at punting should actually have cured me for life, but they didn't. Still, even today as a gambler I'm a very small investor compared to the other author of this book.

Going back to 1968, I must tell you how I started. John Gleeson, our mystery spinner, had devised a system which he reckoned was going to make us a fortune on the roulette tables around the UK. It wasn't quite a double-up system but it was pretty close to it. Like a lot of other systems it did look good on paper. We had to wait for three of a kind on any even-money bet, then hit the wheel. It could be red or black, odds or evens, unders or overs, etc, and then the theory was that we should back the opposite. On consideration now that already sounds less than smart, as most will tell you that you should back with the wheel and not against it. We actually wanted to lose the first three or four and then collect our rewards on the fifth, sixth or seventh spins. The seventh spin, however, was cutting a very fine line. If we should happen to miss eight times in a row, we were out of business.

Anyway, to a group of novice punters it sounded pretty good and John managed to convince Ian Chappell, Dave Renneberg, Brian Taber and myself that we should at least give it a try. We attacked the Golden Nugget Club in London on the second day after our arrival. We gave up a stint at the front bar of the Waldorf, although it didn't turn out that we were away all that long.

We piled into a big, black taxi and spent about two pounds getting to the Casino. When we hopped out and tipped the driver ten pence, he threw it out the window muttering something that sounded like 'miserable Aussies'. We didn't have a lot of money and we weren't used to tipping, so didn't realize that he would expect more for the ride. As it was, we had pooled our meal allowances for about three weeks to give this great system a try. Maybe he would do better on our return journey if everything went as planned.

Twenty pounds each was our starting figure. We carefully chose a table and approached it with our scorecards in hand and waited for our big moment. John Gleeson was the scorer and Ian Chappell was in charge of the bets, while Dave, Brian and myself were spectators-cum-security guards. Our first opportunity didn't take too long to arrive. Three blacks bobbed up on the scorecard. The bets were in 25-pence chips at that stage, but for even-money bets the minimum was 50 pence.

John gave the order to hit the reds, Ian obliged, and we had immediate success. Great, we were a whole 50 pence richer. We were thinking it was going to be very easy pickings.

We had a few more small collects on even money chances and were just waiting to have a big plunge. Alas, however, we were again on reds when eight blacks in a row were recorded on the card. We just couldn't believe the system had failed and we stood there shaking our heads. We kept score till the sequence ended, and would you believe, there were seventeen blacks in a row. Wow, that really rubbed insult into our injury, and we were off out the door.

However, we had a quick conference on the footpath about our bad luck and ended up convinced that the sequence we had watched just a short while before could not possibly happen again. When it was found that someone in the group had more cash on them, we borrowed and decided to invest another 20 pounds each. Back through the door we went, and this time thought that we wouldn't go anywhere near the croupier who had just ripped us off for a hundred quid. We settled on a table on the other side of the room and began again with the same scorer, same person placing the bets, and the same security.

This time we were on the colour which had just been our downfall, the blacks. We didn't have to hang around in suspense for too long, because eight reds put us straight back out of business. We did score the remaining 21 reds in a row, making a staggering 29 in total. In hindsight, this gives some credence to the system of backing with the wheel rather than against it.

'Imagine! Two hundred quid! I'd hardly even earned that much in my life,' I was thinking as we were walking back to the Waldorf. I even gave some thought to going back to check whether the 10 pence the taxi driver had thrown at us was still lying on the footpath. This was not a great start to my gambling career, and our next meal allowance payment was not due for another fortnight.

Well, even the Waldorf must have taken credit in those days, as it was too late to cash in any traveller's cheques but we still drowned our sorrows in the bar that night. It seemed we'd only been away from it for an hour when we walked back in. We didn't eat very well for the next month either. We found hamburgers around the corner were more within our budget than the steaks we would have liked to consume at the Hansom Grill.

Frank Russell who owned the Cricketers' Club of London was very good to us. He shouted us a number of Swan beers and some meals as well. His club was like a home away from home, and we met some great people on our visits there. Denis Compton, the renowned English batsman, spent a lot of time there. I think his reasons for being there were far from those of our broke punting team. Frank actually enjoyed a bet as well, and often after closing his club, he took us to one of the more exclusive casinos where he had a little dabble. Of course, we were only there as spectators.

However, another interest was developing for me. Apart from being good company and generous with drinks and meals, Frank loved his horses, and the coverage on BBC television was pretty good. A bonus was that he convinced us that we should have a little interest along with him, and he covered our outlay on his account. This became an interesting contest for me. We had only just got a television at home, a black-and-white set, and here I was in London watching live horseracing on colour television. Well I hadn't seen colour on television before, and with Frank's tips, I started to claw my way back to square. My first venture into gambling on horses earned me a profit of two pounds. I thought, 'Now I only have 38 to go'.

On that tour, Barry Jarman was our vice-captain and number-one keeper. At that stage he was about the only member of the team who actually followed horses and I decided to keep him within earshot whenever I was tempted again. We actually went to a couple of race meetings with Frank, and, little by little, I regained the money I had lost at my first dabble at a casino. I wasn't in the big league and fortunately, still to this day, I'm still only a small punter, although now very keen.

I've learned over the years that the secret is to get as much information as you possibly can. I'm so keen now that, as I write, I am listening to 2KY Racing Radio 1314 on my transistor as it comes live from Wollongong, which is about 100 kilometres away from my home in Sydney.

My love of gambling has graduated mainly to the gallops, although that doesn't mean I won't also have a bet on the dogs, trotters or, for that matter, two flies walking up a wall. There has been a lot written and a lot more spoken about cricketers and betting on cricket matches over the last couple of years. Well I must tell you that once, and only once, I was tempted to have a bet during a cricket match that I was actually playing in. It happened in England again but this time during the 1972 tour. Ladbrokes, who operate betting tents around the Test matches over there, had decided that there was enough interest in the Australia v Yorkshire match to operate during this game.

The first of the scheduled three days had been washed out so the two official bodies decided that it would be better to play two one-day matches instead. Yes, one-day cricket was played back in those days—but it was a little different to the way it is played now. Dennis Lillee was elected to carry the drinks for the first match, and Ian Chappell won the toss. The wicket was still rain-affected so he sent Yorkshire in to bat.

We had them in a little trouble at 4 for 40 after the first hour, although Geoff Boycott was still in. He had opened the innings and had played in his usual whirlwind style, as evidenced by the fact that he was 2 not out at this stage. I was fielding at fine-leg, which was right outside the Ladbrokes tent, when Dennis Lillee, our twelfth man, walked out the front door.

111

He said, 'You blokes are 12 to 1 about getting five wickets in this session'. I had a quick glance at the scoreboard and realized that we still had an hour and a half until lunch. This convinced me that I should have an interest, at these odds. 'There just happens to be 20 in my trousers pocket in the dressing room, put it on for me,' I replied. At the completion of that over I hurried to the centre of the wicket to inform Rod Marsh, who I thought might also be interested. He didn't even glance at the score-board, let alone the clock. 'Get 20 on for me as well,' he said. Now, Ian Chappell, our inquisitive captain, wanted to know what tactics we were discussing, so we had to inform him. After carefully doing his sums, Ian said he wanted 20 as well. Next thing, his brother Greg arrived. Greg didn't exactly share our confidence, as he only wanted 15. Well, would you believe that word spreads pretty quickly around a cricket field?

After the first ball of the next over had been bowled, I heard a shout of 'Twenty!' from third man. The next delivery was followed with a shout of 'Twenty!' from fine-leg, a 'Ten!' from backward square, and another 'Twenty!' from mid-on. By the time the over had ended everyone had made their call.

I quickly did my sums and headed back to fine-leg near the Ladbrokes tent. At the same time Dennis was just arriving back with our twenties in his hand. I told him that he needed to go back to the dressing room to find some more money because the whole team was now interested in the odds. Well Dennis obliged and gave us the thumbs-up signal to let us know that we were all set. We really got down to business then and we tried like hell to get that fifth wicket. It finally happened about half an hour before lunch. Boycott's middle stump went cartwheeling back a few yards.

Normally on a cricket field when a middle stump is knocked out you don't see 11 fielders appealing, and in this case we actually had 12 because Dennis was up on the balcony giving us a hand as well. By lunchtime Yorkshire were 6 for 62. Ashley

Mallett had pulled off another one of those near impossible chances he often took in the gully. Everyone was doing their 12-times tables as they hurried off the ground to find Dennis. Dennis wasn't exactly a good twelfth man. I don't think he'd had the job before and I don't think he's had it since. He wasn't waiting for us on our arrival. He was already in the lunchroom. He had half finished his lunch when we asked for our money. 'I haven't been down to collect it yet,' replied Dennis. Well the boys demanded that he should go down immediately and get it, and Dennis obliged. He came back in a short while, shaking his head.

'Sorry boys,' he said. 'I've got some bad news for you.'

'What do you mean, bad news?' I asked. 'You said we were on odds of 12 to 1 about getting five wickets in a session, and we've actually done better than that, we've got six!'

'Yeah, that's where you made your mistake,' he replied. 'The bet was for five not six!' My one and only cricket bet had ended as badly as our roulette escapade four years earlier.

I must say, I do believe that sports people should not bet on games that they are playing in. After the 500 to 1 bet nine years later that Rod Marsh and Dennis Lillee were alleged to be involved in, the cricket controlling body has banned its players from doing so.

At the moment I'm actually contracted to City Index in Australia. This company takes bets on everything to do with sport, however, my being 'on the staff' prevents me from betting on cricket here in Australia. The very same information my co-author has been accused of accepting money for is required on a daily basis by City Index, but, I hasten to add that we don't pay individuals for this service.

Like most punters, I have all the usual unlucky tales to tell of what could have been, 'if only'. I probably have more bet-ting systems than any other punter, but putting them together correctly so that everything coincides to make a good day is something that rarely happens. I end up with markings and numbers written all over my form guides. I sometimes colour-code them as well, but half the time I end up talking myself out of winners.

Some of my systems include backing horses on their third run back from a spell, double numbers, which means finishing in the same place in the last two runs. For example, I will check whether a horse finishes fourth in its last two starts, fifth in its last two starts, etc. A third system is when a horse has only one run and is then given a spell. I would back that same horse when it next starts. My preferred system is to back horses that have won three starts back in the same preparation and have then been unplaced in their next two starts. The odds are normally good, and they generally give you a good sight. This system has produced my only 100 to 1 winners and I must tell you they have been few and far between. If there aren't any horses that qualify for this system in the races of the day, I always write down the first four horses in paper-betting order and back one of them. This system obviously supplies more winners as those market makers provide many more wins than all the professional tipsters put together. I have only ever tried these systems at the gallops, not the trots or on the dogs. I usually end up having a bet on every race everywhere when I bet, and my outlays in the races can range from betting on a win and place, to doubles, trifectas, exactas, quinellas, parlays, the lot. I'm frequently told that I can't make money that way, and I always reply, 'I've found that out'.

My favourite horses go back to Tulloch and Kingston Town, and, more currently, Might and Power. Malcolm Johnston, who rode Kingston Town on many of his wins, is a mate of mine. I could laugh all day at the stories he tells, and sometimes I do, as we frequently work together. My favourite of his stories relates to the fact that he was given more than 50 suspensions during his riding career, and he had used many different excuses for his misdemeanours, when he was called before the stewards yet again.

He was asked to explain why his mount had shifted out, almost knocking a couple of horses over. His excuse on this occasion was that a seagull had flown across his path and his horse had shied after seeing it. 'Is that so?' queried the Chief Steward. 'We'll replay the race right now, and see if you have a case.' Of course the television replay revealed no seagull, and he was questioned again about the race. 'What do you have to say now?' Still not lost for words Malcolm replied, 'You don't think the bloody thing would still be there now do you?' Of course a suspension ensued, and three weeks later Mal resumed his riding career.

Malcolm also tells a great story about Kingston Town as a youngster. The late T.J. Smith, the great man of racing, trained the horse and was overseas at the time of his first run. Ernie, his brother, was in charge of the horse and had questioned Mal after his early morning track work. 'How's that black horse going Malcolm?' he asked. 'Oh, he's going really well, Ernie. There's something special about him,' Mal replied. Ernie said that he wanted Malcolm to give the horse another hit out following Saturday morning, as he was racing on the Wednesday after. Then Ernie added that they might be able to have a bet. Ernie loved a bet, and 'The King' trialled well on the Saturday morning. They were then looking forward to Wednesday.

Malcolm always says that jockeys can't bet, but his wife had a substantial plunge on that day. Ernie had obviously outlayed a fair whack too, because as Malcolm went to the birdcage, he noticed that the price had shortened a couple of points, and the horse would now start as firm favourite. They were full of anticipation for the great things to come as the horses went to the barriers, but when the barriers crashed back, Kingston Town missed the start. Malcolm says that it is pretty serious business to try and make up four lengths over a short distance race. He produced the whip, only to slip even further behind.

Yes, Kingston Town tailed off last. The further they had raced the further he slipped behind.

Now, Malcolm wasn't looking forward to the reception he knew he was about to get from Ernie. He could see Ernie wasn't a happy man as he had dribble coming out of his nose and betting tickets flying out of his pockets. 'What the so-and-so happened to that bloody horse?' he asked. Malcolm had used as many excuses to the trainers as he had used to the stewards, so he had to think really quickly to answer this unhappy man. 'I think he needs gelding,' Mal replied as quick as a wink. As Ernie tossed more betting tickets out of his pockets, he turned away and he said, 'I know who needs bloody gelding, and it's not the horse'.

Malcolm adds that sometimes jockeys fluke the correct answers—Kingston Town was gelded early the next morning. The great T.J. didn't have any say in it either, but it probably proved to be the right decision—Kingston Town won 19 straight races on city tracks after that first-up failure. Mal didn't complete the story by telling me if his wife had backed up with her money on those races but I'm sure Ernie would have had his money there.

I've met many big and colourful gamblers over the years, but have noticed that not many of them live in huge houses or drive expensive cars. The bookmakers and the TAB are the big winners, but that won't stop us trying to reach that magic day when the systems all work. I guess we all like to dream it will happen one day.

IT'S IN THE BLOOD

*'Apart from that more serious betting, I also have a
running bet with Shane Warne which is a bit of fun.'*

Punting and horseracing have always been in my blood. I'm sure
it all comes from my grandfather originally. He was a very keen
punter, and lived in Ballina opposite the racecourse. He went to
the races every week, even in his eighties. That's almost certainly
where my love of horse racing and the trots started.

Whenever I went on holidays to visit him the first thing we
did was go over the race fields in the paper with a fine-tooth
comb. Grandfather loved his sport, having been a representative league player and a trainer of greyhounds.

Stephen, on the other hand, would rarely have a punt even
though we grew up in exactly the same way. So I guess it's
always been a part of me from the time I was seven and dad
took the family to the Bankstown trots. I absolutely loved it

117

from that day. Dad gave us a dollar so I studied the form and placed the bet. We were given a race each on which to win our fortune. I can't recall my first winner, but it must have been a good one because I've been hooked ever since.

It's a relaxation for me. When I'm at the races I don't think about anything else. I can go by myself and never worry about being alone or think of anything but the races. I can literally spend hours there studying the form and having a bet. I don't take any notice of anyone else. I don't even talk to the person I might have gone with. I bet and watch the passing parade or I'll go to the stables and look at the horses. I just love everything about it. There's something exciting about horses just as animals. They're so athletic and strong. Very well put together. A combination of power and athleticism with perfect balance.

Owning a few horses—a few trotters—has opened up a whole new perspective, making it very exciting. Most of the guys in the team find it really boring. Only Ricky Ponting, Darren Lehmann and myself like the horses. We're forever in the dressing rooms on a rainy day wanting to watch the races and the others are always changing the channel. We turn it on and they turn it off. I guess it's something you either love or hate.

I'm very interested in the breeding and training too. Whenever I can I go down to Exeter, NSW, where my horses are based with the Glenn Frost Stable, and spend quite a bit of time talking about how they're going. I don't get down there too often, of course, but I love to look into the training and breeding side of things too. I can see some sort of future in all of this but I also think I'll end up working somewhere around cricket when I retire. The cricket still comes first.

The only problem is that I'm allergic to horse hair. It's a big problem for someone with an interest as strong as mine. It's like being a cricketer who's allergic to grass. Every time I go to see my horses I have to take tablets or I'm a mess—runny nose, runny eyes.

I've made a lot of friends through the racing and trotting game. I like to go to Sydney's Harold Park whenever I can on Friday nights and sit in the Committee Room where I have some really good friends. Two of my best friends are the bosses at Harold Park, Peter V'Landys and John Dumesny, and when I'm overseas they send me faxes—race clippings and things about other sports. They keep me up-to-date, which I really appreciate. We get looked after so well in the Committee Room they even peel our prawns for us. It's always such a great night of entertainment.

When we're overseas on tour I try to get to the races. I went with Ricky to the races in Barbados. It was the Barbados Cup, which was fantastic. There was a carnival atmosphere and it was something like a picnic day for them. It was very funny with people walking down the main straight and across it. There were games being played on the infield and it was so different from what we're used to here. Very relaxed. I always try and get to the race tracks around the world. I like to compare the quality of the horses and the different approaches to racing generally. It's also a real escape when we're on tour.

I've seen races at Ascot in England, Auckland in New Zealand, Durban in South Africa and Calcutta in India. All were unique in their own way. To me, however, Australia still has the best facilities and horses.

My biggest price ever, which was not my biggest win, was when I was 17. It was at Canterbury racetrack and I went down to the stables between races. Peter Sterling, the rugby league footballer, was there with a horse I think he had an interest in. It was called Long John Silver—a big grey horse—and I thought, 'I'll go and back that'. It was at 150 to 1, and as luck would have it Long John Silver led all the way and won like an odds-on chance. The only reason I backed it was because Peter Sterling was one of my heroes.

My favourite horse of all time was Super Impose. I love the way it would come from last on the turn and flash home. What a great racehorse! I backed it in the Cox Plate when it won at 25 to 1. That was one of my biggest ever wins. I had a good bet on it but I won't tell you how much. I've had some decent wins in my time but I reckon I'd still be just behind overall. Another win of his I will never forget was in the Doncaster at Randwick when he came from stone motherless last and whizzed home past 23 horses in the straight to win running away.

You've got to do something with your money and you must have an interest outside of cricket. I'd rather buy a racehorse than a car, whereas a lot of the guys on the team will spend all their money on a car. It's the thought of one day owning a horse that could win the Melbourne Cup or the Inter Dominion that keeps me wanting to buy horses. I just want that one brilliant horse.

I've also had trotters. I've won seven races in three months with them. They were both Kiwi pacers, and one in particular, Oblico, is a very promising pacer. He's won 7 from 15 and I'm sure there are plenty more wins left in him. At present a serious leg injury has sidelined him but a full recovery will see a very good horse develop. It is amazing how nervous you can get when your horse is racing. It's a mixture of excitement, anticipation and apprehension, hoping he'll win and not have a mishap during the race. It's all good fun.

I have people in New Zealand who keep an eye out for good horses for me. One day I'll find the champion. I'm also involved in the gallopers with a syndicate called Sports Star Syndications. They're an organisation that give sports stars a share in a horse to attract other people to join the syndicate. We have a couple of young horses that haven't raced yet under the scheme but they're looking good.

When I was in England in 1997 my horse Clever Kiwi was racing in Sydney at Fairfield. It was 11.00am in England, and we were playing Nottinghamshire in a county game. Ricky was batting with Matthew Elliott and I was next in. I warned Ricky,

120

'Whatever you do, don't get out in the first over because the race is on at 11.00am.' I was in the toilet phoning home on the mobile and, just as Sue answered the phone, I heard 'Howzat!' I hung on till about 500 metres to go. My horse was running second and by this time Ricky was given out LBW and was walking off. Finally I had to go in, so I hung up with about 30 seconds to go. It ran fourth. I know this story will be used against me at some point, but that's exactly what happened. You're not supposed to use mobile phones from the time you leave the hotel until you return, but sometimes you just have to, especially in emergencies.

When I backed Super Impose in the Cox Plate, the race was on at 3.00pm and I was playing grade cricket at the time at Sydney University. Stephen and I were batting and the only way to watch the race was to get out or win the game very quickly. We only needed 30 to win. It was going to be easy with Stephen smashing them and I already had 40-odd. I wouldn't say I tried to get out but I played an optimistic stroke. I was caught in the deep and I charged up to one of the Sydney Uni bars to watch the race. It was well planned because we won the game in a canter, and Super Impose won an action-packed Cox Plate.

No matter how all this might sound, my greater love is still cricket, and I can honestly say I would never put my team or my cricket second. Punting really is a pure relaxation for me. I'm not a gambler as such. I would rarely bet in a casino, or on cards, machines or dogs. Mainly the races and trots. I do occasionally bet on sport, as has been widely reported—never cricket, just rugby league, tennis and golf. I think I know a bit about sport and for me betting on it is an interest. I don't bet every day either. It is not a compulsion for me, just an every-second-day hobby.

I have had a bit of luck on sports betting, especially on rugby league and golf. Mark O'Meara winning the British Open in 1998 was a big result. From memory I secured 50 to 1 with my

121

good mate Gerard Daffy at Centrebet and watched O'Meara win the Open in a tense playoff. The previous year Jesper Parnevik teased me for days, just about leading all the way then faltering on the last few holes. At 80 to 1 each way, I still ended up making a quid.

Canterbury Bankstown rugby league, who I support with immense pride and passion, get my money nearly every week. This could be called betting with your heart and not your head but the 1998 season saw the Bulldogs finish with a remarkable string of wins and a place in the Grand Final. I was fortunate enough to ride in on that winning wave—making some cash week after week.

Apart from that more serious betting I also have a running bet with Shane Warne which is a bit of fun. It involves champion fast bowler Glenn McGrath but has nothing to do with his bowling. It's his batting, in fact, that absorbs our attention. The bet is whether he can score a first-class 50. I believe with his ability with the stick he can't possibly! But Warnie's always good for a light-hearted argument and he thinks he can. So far the closest Glenn has come was in the first Test in the West Indies in 1999 in Trinidad where he made a splendidly organised 39. I must admit that, with the West Indies bowlers tiring on a flat pitch, I was thinking that the miracle would occur.

Fortunately for my bank balance the natural order prevailed and Glenn became over confident, nicking a cover drive to the keeper. Mind you, I would have been more than happy to see things go Warnie's way, as it would have been well worth it to see a number 11 get 50 against the might of Ambrose, Walsh and co. By the way, just in case anyone wants to take this light-hearted wager out of context, rest assured that if either of us ever collects the $1,000, it will be going to charity.

CHAPTER EIGHT

THE MEDIA

RADIO DAYS AND
BACKYARD CRICKET

*'When we played our "Test matches" as children, our side
verandah became the wonderful fields the commentators
described.'*

We know that without media there would be no sport, as there
would be nobody to watch it. Whether you like or dislike the
media, it is a part of our life. It is difficult to imagine how we
would get by not knowing what was going on in the world. We
may enjoy going without television, radio and newspapers for a
few days every now and again, but I'm sure that if it went on
for too long we would all have withdrawal symptoms and want
to return to knowing world news as it breaks.

All forms of media are equally important, and I have found
that media people vary a great deal, just as people do in all
walks of life. The majority of media people are great. They have

a job to do, as does everyone else, but sometimes this is forgotten. It is said that the media can 'make or break' you. This is true, but I think the media makes more than it breaks. If you get offside with the media you need to make sure that you don't make any mistakes for the rest of your life because the poison pen is definitely mightier than the sword and the whole world will quickly know all about your mistakes.

I have always had a good relationship with the press and have frequently enjoyed the company of people in the media along with my sporting friends. Some people find it difficult to accept criticism, but if it's the truth, there isn't much you can do about it. It is obvious that some journalists can talk about poor shots in a kinder way than others. Some choose to ignore mistakes completely.

Of course it is easier to appreciate the latter if you are the person who has played the poor shot, but you can't hide from people watching your mistakes on camera. Television viewers always have tremendous memories and this form of media allows the real wags in the crowd to come to the fore. People will come up to you and say all sorts of things about the way you play. Spectators seldom forget either, so I have found it is better to just give them a wave or have a laugh with them than to take offense.

On an overseas tour the media are regarded as part of the touring party and are often invited to many player functions as well as enjoying many of the privileges that players are offered. As a player I always thought that I needed all the help I could get, particularly in foreign countries where it is always good to hear an Australian accent. Some players have mentioned that they think journalists are only around to hear a major scoop. In reality there are very few who have these intentions.

These days, however, there are some parts of the media looking for any form of scandal. These people do need sorting out, but they are usually not too hard to find. In the past, I have noticed that many cricketers have found jobs in the media once they retired from playing and it is amazing how, when their perspective changes from player to commentator, their opinions can suddenly change, seemingly overnight. It is a good way to remain involved in the game and there are many opportunities, particularly in television, as these days there are a number of different forms of television coverage of matches on free-to-air and pay TV.

More recently there has been an even greater number of retired and current players actively involved in various forms of media around the world. I have found that their articles, and thoughts on television are mostly very refreshing, and I feel that these are the people who should know what they're talking about. It's just as well we don't all think alike. Having different opinions means that we all can enjoy discussions and arguments at the pub as we study the replays.

When I was playing state and Australian cricket, prior to contracts with the Cricket Board, it was illegal for players to write articles in the press. I think the recent changes have been for the better. Players would hardly write articles that openly abuse officials or their own team-mates. Also, they wouldn't want to jeopardize their own careers, so it was always a controversial restriction. I think that players who fear the media have a problem, and it would be a good idea if they didn't read the newspaper reports, or watch television reports, for that matter. Such players don't tend to last in the sport for too long.

At times, some members of the media tend to get too close to players too soon after they have been dismissed. Of course these players are hardly going to be happy. When World Series Cricket started the practice of interviewing players as soon as they got out began. As it turned out, many players frequently wished they could take back the things they said in the heat of the moment. They wouldn't have said half the things they did, once they had a chance to cool off.

I grew up listening to radio. Names like Alan McGilvray,

Johnnie Moyes, Charles Fortune, John Arlott and Brian Johnston come instantly to my mind. I loved this form of media, as these commentators would describe everything. When we played our 'Test matches' as children, our side verandah became the wonderful fields the commentators described. We commentated in the voices we had heard during the night as we played through the actions of our heroes. We were right-or left-handers, had stuttered run ups, or had a flourish with the bat. We copied them in every way they were described. There was no television in Australia at that stage, but these radio commentators painted such wonderful images of players in our minds we could tell who all the kids were copying and who we were playing against. Kids still do this today.

When I'm coaching, I can tell who the kids are emulating from the television. Of course the television makes it easier for the kids now, but I feel that the great voices of radio were just as good. I actually got to play with and against some of my heroes in later life. I was amazed to see that their actions resembled mine. Maybe it was the other way around because we aped every word. I didn't have a pair of brown and white shoes like Brian Johnston was described as wearing, but if I did, I would have worn them as we played.

I couldn't believe my eyes when I actually met 'Johnners' in England in 1968. He wasn't wearing his famous shoes. We were playing a county game when I met him and I had to ask him about these shoes. 'Douggers,' he said, 'brown and whiters are for Testers only.' Sure enough, when we played the Test in Manchester he was there with the shoes on. They looked as if they had been all polished up for the occasion. We miss having these great characters today, but time moves on, and there are already other characters taking their places.

I enjoyed radio far more than television when I dabbled into match commentary as a media employee. I worked for Radio 2UE in Sydney and, later, 4BC in Brisbane when they were doing ball by ball commentary at the Test matches and one-day games. We had a great team of fellows working at these matches. We actually had too many in the team, as it eventually proved uneconomical. In the radio media you can have more to say and the freedom to say it; 2UE is a commercial station, but we still fitted in our ads around the commentary.

Television seemed to have constant interruptions for ads, and I found this annoying as a commentator, just as I do as a viewer. I couldn't come to grips with television at all, particularly when directors wanted to replay things like wides from three or four different angles rather than let me finish what I had been saying. I actually feel that television needs little commentary since people are already watching the match. Some television commentary almost sounds as if it is scripted, and you can almost predict what commentators are going to say, particularly the one-day games.

We will miss Richie Benaud when he decides to retire from commentary. In my opinion, he has brought as much to television commentary as the other great names I was talking about brought to radio.

The late Ray Robinson was probably my favourite journalist of all time, and he was well respected and liked by all the other players I mixed with. Ray wrote articles for the Sydney paper the *Daily Mirror*, and it was always a pleasure to read his work. I found it inspirational as well. Ray never wrote a bad word about anyone and he didn't mention incidents at times when other writers were getting headlines from them. He was always welcome in our dressing rooms and he would have heard many scoops that he never chose to release. The dressing-room door attendants were selective about who they let in, as they also read the papers and were very protective of the players. I guess they still do the same job.

Cec Davies was our room attendant for many years in Sydney. He could never be replaced. He would never hear a bad word about anyone and I think he enjoyed the hard times we gave him. He was part of our team, and there were lots of times when we would love to have sent him out to bat for us, even though he was in his eighties at the time. The boys would constantly rib him about the tea being too cold and about weevils in the biscuits that he had bought out of his own pocket, but none of these things would phase Cec. Our boots, pads, etc would always be immaculately cleaned every day, whether they had been worn or not. I'd love to have him with us now.

Every state had a man like Cec. There was actually an attendant in each dressing room, and each assigned attendant was loyal to the team in the dressing room he was in, even if they were playing against his home state. These attendants loved their cricket, but if the press got past them, then you knew they were okay.

I am certain that we need all forms of media to keep promoting the great game of cricket, and, overall, I feel that the journalists have done a good job. If we didn't have personalities in the media then comedians like Billy Birmingham ('The Twelfth Man') would lack the material to entertain us. I think that Richie Benaud even enjoys some of the humour in Billy's tapes. Sometimes I think that he takes off some of the commentators so well, you really can't tell the real voices from his own.

A FINE LINE TO TREAD

*'All through my career, various journalists have said
I could give more. I know I'm doing my best. Why on earth
wouldn't I do my best when there's so much at stake?'*

I have always kept in mind, even when really fed up, that the
media have a job to do too. I really try to remember that. The
media is so much a part of the life of an international cricketer
that you have to respect the fact that they have a job to do just
as we have a job to do. Naturally we benefit in many, many
ways from media attention but there is a price to pay.

Up to a point, I can even accept media criticism when it's
warranted, and it has been warranted from time to time. Of
course there'll be criticism, and you take it on the chin if it's fair
criticism even though it's hard. I can accept it even more readily
from a journalist or TV commentator who has played the game.

What I really can't stand, though, and find hard to accept, is when a journalist is writing about how I'm playing when they clearly have no understanding of the intricacies of the game. Sometimes they're writing uninformed opinions for a very wide audience. At least half of the audience will believe what they read. That disturbs me a little—when a cricket expert from the media who has never played the game starts offering opinions on something he has never encountered himself.

It can be very difficult for a player to shake a tag which is given to them by an established cricket writer. Take Michael Bevan, for example. It is often written that he can't play short-pitch bowling and he'll never be a good Test player because of it. I've seen him play many games throughout NSW and Australia, and he's made many runs against the West Indies. I know for a fact he can play short pitch bowling and I've seen him do it very well many times. But invariably you'll pick up a paper and read that he can't play short pitch bowling and there-fore will never be a Test player. I think Michael now believes that himself to a certain extent, and he shouldn't.

The people who write these comments have probably never played a short-pitch ball or know how to do it themselves. In the majority of cases they've probably never played a serious game of cricket. No wonder they come to such wrong conclusions. This sort of reporting can break players. If a player is not mentally tough or is just starting out, negative media will really get him down and doubting himself. I believe that, in this way, the media can and often do have a say in determining the shape of a player's career. Even selectors can be swayed in judgement if they read something often enough. On the other hand, the media can also build players up and that can obviously help a player's confidence.

Overall, the media have written the same things about my cricket for many years. I'll constantly read that I'm too casual or don't care enough about what I'm doing. The truth of the matter is exactly the opposite. I try as hard as anybody.

With Stephen, you read that he's the tough, gritty competitor—that he never gives an inch, which of course is true. But I know that I'm just as competitive as Stephen. It's all just a perception based on visual appearance. I look as if I'm casual and as if I'm doing it all easily, but in fact, I'm giving a hundred per cent and I don't find it at all easy.

All through my career, various journalists have said I could give more. I know I'm doing my best. Why on earth wouldn't I do my best when there's so much at stake? I've carried that 'casual, lazy' tag for years, a bit like England's David Gower. It just isn't true.

Certainly it has softened a little over the years. I've played some very important innings more recently, so the tags haven't been thrown around as much. In Port Elizabeth, for example, where I made 100 and we won the game, and in Adelaide against South Africa where I got 100-odd not out and we drew the game with me batting for the whole last day. Those and other successes have slightly changed the media perception of me, but still the bandwagon keeps rolling along with cries of how I could have done a lot better. It is said that losing or getting out doesn't hurt me enough. My response to that, now that I have an opportunity to respond, is to say, just because I don't wear my heart on my sleeve doesn't mean I don't feel the losses deeply. I feel it just as much as the other players.

I also don't wear the baggy green cap all the time, and it has been suggested in the media that this shows I don't take as much pride in playing for Australia as some other players do who always wear them. This sort of speculation is nonsense. I don't need to wear the baggy green cap to have pride in my country. I feel great pride anyway.

I know Mike Coward has written along these lines from time to time, and sometimes Peter Roebuck's articles have suggested I might be more interested in the races at Randwick when I'm standing out there batting, instead of concentrating on the cricket. There have also been suggestions made by various journalists that I don't think about the game much. Yet I know that I have as good a cricket brain as anyone in the team and I think about the game as much as anybody.

The idea that if I go out there and have a good day then it's a matter of chance is ridiculous; that I am thinking about racing and not cricket is ridiculous. I do love racing but I also know how to separate the two things. I would never have made it this far if I couldn't completely focus. This sort of comment indicates that those writing such opinions don't know what it takes to stand out there in the middle and concentrate.

The only way you can deal with such irritating and incorrect reporting is to keep getting runs, but then I get the comments that I'm doing it easily. People read stories and then ask me, 'So why did you get out? You looked like you were doing it easily.' You can't win.

Sometimes I have confronted journalists. Mike Coward wrote a story about me when I was in Pakistan, saying that my place in the side was in jeopardy coming into the third Test. I just don't know how he worked that one out. I'd made a duck in the first Test and then 40-odd in the second. Before that I'd made three centuries out of my last six Tests so I had genuinely thought that I was doing pretty well.

Coward wrote something along the lines of 'if Mark Waugh fails in this Test then I think he's a big chance of being dropped'. I was pretty cross. My record in the previous year in Test cricket was an average of somewhere around 60, so I just couldn't work out how he came to the conclusion that my spot was under pressure. I spoke to him on a plane in India and I told him that when we arrived I wanted to chat with him in private. I really wanted to know how he had formed his opinion. Unfortunately, I didn't catch up with him because he went home.

I do think players should speak to journalists if a story that's been written is purely speculative, unfounded or untrue. It can be so damaging. I think it is important that we find out what a journalist is thinking in such circumstances.

The Australian team has also suffered from the fact that journalists, particularly those overseas, continually conclude we are sledgers. At very worst, I would say we play tough cricket which involves gamesmanship rather than out-and-out sledging. Whenever there is an on-field incident it is more often than not written up as our doing. This tag, no matter what we say or do is one we can't shake.

Perhaps journalists are writing news and need some juicy headlines but often they are way off the mark. I do try to read as much as possible of what's written about the team. We all do. It's human nature to want to know what's being said about you, even though you probably shouldn't in a lot of cases. I always have the papers saved for me when I'm travelling and usually the ACB will fax clippings to us. We're always keen to know what's being written at home.

Having said all that, I don't think the front page of serious newspapers should carry stories about whether someone's a chucker or not. Surely there are more important things going on in the world? To me cricket is a sport. I know many people follow it, but it shouldn't push stories of war and natural disaster off the front pages. It's not more important than the welfare of people in Australia and around the world. It's not as important as pressing social issues. If a guy has a bent or straight arm, or was given a black eye in a nightclub, is it so important that it pushes all political matters aside in the media? To run such incidents as lead stories is, in my opinion, going overboard.

Putting cricketers on a pedestal is not healthy. We're supposed to be perfect human beings, and any fall from grace becomes major news. We're like anyone else. We make mistakes too. Sometimes we get so built up and so knocked down that everything we do becomes exaggerated and out of perspective.

Certainly we are role models for younger fans, and there wouldn't be a player who doesn't take that into consideration, but we're also human and have emotions. We're not the only role models. What about their peers, their parents and the stuff kids see these days on television and the internet? Overall, I don't think the cricketers set too bad an example.

When we're on tour, journalists live very closely with the cricket team. In Pakistan they're on the same bus and in the same hotel. If we tour to look at a tourist spot, the journalists come with us on our bus. Down at practice they'll kick our footy around with us after the training is finished. We talk in the bar together, if there's not much happening. In the past we haven't been guarded or particularly careful with our talk but now there's nothing said off the cuff when you're talking to a media person. They always have their ears open and we are careful about making comments that could be blown up or taken out of context.

Overall, though, the relationship is pretty good. I haven't had very many complaints to make over the years. Naturally, there are lines that neither steps over.

On the other hand, there are journalists I'd never talk to again after some of the things that were written about me during the so called 'Bookie Scandal'. The whole team was amazed at how things were twisted and changed in the media.

I can't help feeling that the Australian press is going a little way towards the state of the English tabloids. Certainly there are good reporters who report accurately on the cricket. Then there are others who dig behind the scenes and try very hard to find something controversial where it doesn't exist. I'm not suggesting there wasn't a real story in the 'Bookie Scandal' but just that it was widely misreported. When the team is doing well, it must be very hard to fill all those column inches.

We do get media training every year and the team is put through hypothetical interviews. We really just need to keep it simple. The media can be very invasive. It has definitely become more so over the years. I am called at home all the time. I take calls but often won't comment. When I first started playing, I assumed that if I was called and asked for an interview I had to participate. Now I don't participate unless it is important or my comments are relevant. You have to draw a line or you'd be doing interviews all the time.

We are obliged to give interviews before a game, and others are specially lined up by our media officer, Patrick Keane. Nine times out of ten I do give interviews, but I am more guarded as the years roll by because I have been misquoted and quoted out of context too often. I also prefer to stay out of the papers when possible.

The media style varies from country to country. In India and Pakistan there seem to be millions of journalists all wanting an interview. They also all want an exclusive and don't like press conference arrangements. You have to be tough, and politely say no more often than yes. We're very conscious of being careful in England where they are always on the look out for the negative spin or controversial angle.

If you ever complain, you're often portrayed as making a fuss or being difficult, and the stories get worse. One Australian journalist even recently asked indignantly if he was only allowed to write about my centuries and shampoo ads when we very politely corrected a specific factual error about me being somewhere at a particular time when I hadn't been. We tried to explain that we were more than happy for the story to run but that his facts were partially wrong.

It's a very tricky business trying to fulfil media engagements, which are definitely part of our job, while still protecting your privacy and the truth of the events which are being reported. I think in any field of work there are people who are good at what they do and others who are not. The print media does include a lot of sound, knowledgeable cricket writers, and all anyone really wants is that they write the truth and request, and respect, the facts. It's the speculation that's so damaging.

Cricket coverage on TV has gone ahead in leaps and bounds. I believe it has definitely lifted the profile of the game and increased the level of interest. In Australia we have coverage equal to that anywhere in the world. By and large, we have tremendous commentators, headed by Richie Benaud. They can bring suspense and excitement to every ball. The camera angles are amazing, picking up every possible movement on the ground including Stumpcam. All those extra slow-motion replays, scoring charts and graphics do add to the spectacle.

Of course we also have cameras following us to airports, hotels, golf courses and training—maybe soon there will be Kitcam or Bagcam! At first it is intrusive but eventually you learn to live with it and then, finally, you find you often don't even notice the cameras. What it does provide is an unprecedented view of the team for the armchair sportsman and that has to be good for the game. I think all the players realise that, for better or worse, media attention is here to stay. The attention is at a height never seen or experienced before, and we'd better get used to it as a regular part of our lives.

CHAPTER NINE

CHANGES TO THE GAME

STILL THE GENTLEMEN'S GAME?

'I was watching a few of the Englishmen and could see that they were smiling because they were thinking they had nailed the great man.'

Since I began my first-class career in the 1962–63 season, lots of changes have taken place both on and off the cricket field. My first game was against Queensland, and opening the bowling for Queensland was one very fast bowler named Wesley Hall. Although he was a West Indian, Wes was playing for Queensland that summer. He didn't get a chance to have a go at me in my first innings as I was bowled neck and crop by Barry Fisher, his opening partner. I scored 50 in the second innings and got to face Wes for several overs. To my absolute amazement I didn't have to duck under one delivery he bowled at me. I'd only just turned 17 at this stage, but I was expecting to have to duck under every second ball as he pushed off from the sight-screen at the SCG.

Years later I asked Wes why he had used this logic in my first game. He replied, 'Man, you were only a boy'. I doubt that being a teenager would carry much weight these days. Cricket was definitely a gentleman's game back then. I'm pleased to report that it still is to a large degree, but all things change as life goes on.

Sure, the bats are still four-and-a-quarter inches wide (10.8 centimetres if you must), the ball is still five-and-a-half ounces (155.9 grams) in weight, and the pitch is still 22 yards (20.12 metres) long. Also, a lot of the rules are exactly the same. When I first started, however, the bowlers were ruled off the back foot. This meant that they couldn't go past the stumps before releasing the ball. It is said that rules are made to be broken, and a lot of bowlers didn't actually bowl from 22 yards. Dragging was very popular, and still is, but the new front-foot law means that they have to start their drag a lot sooner.

Gordon Rorke was one of our opening bowlers for NSW in 1962–63, and he had the most amazing drag of all time. In fact, he had two or three drags coupled with a giant stride when releasing the ball. Eighteen yards would probably be a fair estimate of the distance he bowled after he released the ball. I think this is why Keith Stackpole, one of Australia's most successful opening batsmen, still says that Rorke was the fastest bowler he ever faced.

Keith opened for Victoria against Rorke in my second Sheffield Shield game, when the SCG was a green top and it was a seaming wicket. He wouldn't have seen the first two balls Gordon bowled, after which Victoria was 0 for 8. Both balls were so wide that they went to the left of the fine-leg fieldsman and into the pickets.

Jeff Thomson was fairly erratic in his early days. He claimed that this gave him an advantage because if he didn't know where the balls were going, the batsmen wouldn't have any chance of knowing either. I reckon if Gordon Rorke and Thommo had opened the bowling together it would have been a nightmare, not only for the opening batsmen, but for the poor wicket-keeper who would inevitably have disastrous figures as well.

Eight-ball overs were bowled in my early days. That was normal in Australia up until the season of 1977–78 when World Series Cricket began. This brought about a number of changes to the game. Six-ball overs became the rule in Australia after World Series Cricket was introduced because that was what was bowled in every other cricketing nation.

If I had a choice, I would like to bowl six-ball overs and bat against eight. I do believe that there were more balls bowled when I started. In fact, I think there were probably even more *overs* bowled with the eight-ball overs than there are these days. More spin bowlers were used in those days too. NSW had wrist spinners like Richie Benaud, Peter Philpott, Johnny Martin, Bob Simpson and Norm O'Neill in the same side.

World Series Cricket brought about the greatest number of changes to our game. Some people were ready for change, but the majority of people around the world were not. The split between the officials of the game and, to some extent, friends (not necessarily players) was obvious from the first day World Series went public. Players had made their decisions in secret. Many people thought that the changes the players voted to undertake would lead to the destruction of the game.

Player payments aside, the decision for me to join World Series Cricket was an easy one. I wasn't getting any younger and had been playing against great opposition from many countries for some years, but I can understand that it would have been a very difficult decision for many younger players. They must have had second thoughts about whether cricket supporters were ready for change, and also the future was looking uncertain at that stage. I am confident that with World Series Cricket the game was given its biggest boost since the career of the great Sir Donald Bradman. Coloured clothing would have remained unheard of and I wonder whether there would have ever been the innovation of playing with white cricket balls under lights at night. At the beginning of World Series Cricket this was like some kind of joke.

By this time Frank Russell, who owned the Cricketers' Club of London, was my good mate, as I had made several tours of England and spent a lot of time with him. My wife travelled to England towards the end of the tours under her own steam on a few occasions. Other wives did the same. Caroline also went to New Zealand under the same arrangements. However, there were times when I managed to stay at her hotel, and at this stage in 1977 Frank and his wife Sheila had offered to have us stay with them.

Their flat was built over the Cricketers' Club we often frequented, and we were pleased to accept their hospitality whenever we were in London. Frank has always boasted that our eldest son, Brynley, was conceived in that flat. I'm not sure whether that was the case or not, but the dates coincide. However, he was born in Sydney, and has an Australian passport.

I was actually staying 'illegally' at Frank and Sheila's flat at this time because prior to World Series Cricket wives were not supposed to belong around cricket grounds, let alone travel overseas to countries where their husbands were touring as part of a cricket team. I'm not arguing that the Cricket Board should have paid wives' expenses, but the rules stated that they couldn't travel with the team under any circumstances, or stay in the same hotel as the team, even if they were paying their own bills.

When the news about World Series Cricket emerged a little prematurely all hell broke loose, but because I wasn't staying at the official accommodation, I took some finding. When we did finally get the news, Frank was very skeptical but from then on he heard a lot about Kerry Packer, and how he was going to 'turn cricket upside down'. This, he most certainly did. Something similar has recently happened in rugby league, but the wounds to that game might take longer to heal than those that were suffered by cricket. It was only two years before Kerry Packer managed to convince the powers that be that the changes he had made were for the better, and the Australian Cricket Board relented. I guess the television rights sealed the deal.

Many players who had signed contracts with World Series Cricket were never heard of again. I was a bit lucky and I just hung on after the reconciliation. I missed a few games but then got back into both the NSW and Australian teams for another short stint. With World Series Cricket the game went into many lounge rooms. Even the skeptics glanced at it and although, I guess, cricket lost a few of its fans, a whole new audience began to enjoy watching. Players became better known to the general public and were more readily recognized everywhere they went.

It seems that many people suddenly feel that they know you personally. I don't really have any complaints about that because, on the whole, I find people are terrific wherever I go and there are very few who make nuisances of themselves. Most are content to say hello and receive an autograph, always for their children, or grandchildren—I find this part a little amusing because my eldest son is now 23 and he hardly remembers me playing any cricket apart from social and charity matches. But perhaps this younger generation are avid readers of the history of the game.

I actually think that World Series Cricket helped the children of cricketers have some interest in the game, as it would have been very difficult to balance a home life if my wife and family had been excluded from being a part of it. In many ways I felt we were lucky not to have had children until the latter stages of my cricket career. As it is, our three sons, Brynley, Lynton and Mitchell, are avid followers of the game. Hannah, our daughter is just as keen.

The portable mikes that were installed around the wicket area with the advent of World Series Cricket have added another dimension to the television coverage of the cricket. Once this began, many Channel 9 technicians had to be really on the ball to keep a step ahead of the players, I can assure you. Nine or ten, sometimes more, cameras have allowed viewers to see every possible angle of the game, and then it can be replayed again and again to promote discussion of the different angles. There can be very little that is missed on or off the playing arena. I suppose some players would still prefer the old system, as nothing is sacred anymore, but it has certainly increased the following and interest in the game from many different spheres of life.

The wickets change from season to season, but generally in Australia, each city apart from Sydney could be expected to have a fairly similar wicket from one year to the next. Some of the other wickets around the world, however, have changed considerably, particularly the English wickets. They became completely covered from the early 1980s. This has made a big difference. It is hard to tell from watching television whether other wickets are now very different. The West Indian wickets look fairly similar to the ones I played on. I think the curators in the West Indies are very even-handed when preparing the pitches. With the bowling attacks they have had, particularly during the late 1970s and early 1980s, one would have thought they'd import grass if they couldn't grow it, yet their pitches have remained good tracks to bat on.

In my opinion, that's the way all wickets should be prepared, and I'm sure Mark will agree with that. Good wickets produce good cricket, and you still get match results. I don't think a game of cricket should be decided on the toss of a coin, as has happened on more than one occasion. Pitches started to change when World Series Cricket began because we were banned from playing on most of the main grounds. 'Hothouse wickets' were grown and transported to grounds such as the VFL Park in

Melbourne, the old Sydney Showground, Football Park in Adelaide, and the Gloucester Park Paceway in Perth. These wickets proved to be a big success. It's actually a pity some of them couldn't be used at the major cricket grounds when the two bodies came together under the control of the Australian Cricket Board.

When Dennis Amiss and Tony Greig appeared wearing the first helmets to be used in cricket, basically motorbike crash helmets, the traditionalists really laughed long and hard. I guess before car seatbelts came in there was a similar response to those, but facts and figures don't lie and new safety features will continue to be improved. As in cricket, many of the current jockeys will tell you that they owe their lives to safety vests they now wear. Close-in fielders have a lot more security now that helmets are an accepted part of the game, as do batsmen who have also incorporated other protective equipment such as chest pads and arm guards. This equipment has not only saved broken bones but also lives, so one can hardly argue about its inclusion.

The introduction of the third umpire and neutral umpires are the latest changes to cricket. I feel these are real benefits to our great game. They have helped settle many arguments. It can no longer be argued that home umpires have made decisions that favoured the local team, or even deliberately cheated. The umpire's decision must be accepted on all occasions—after all, he is never wrong once it is written in the score book, but to my mind these changes have been for the best.

Another reason why I have always accepted the umpire's decision is that I've never wanted to be one. I often chat to them and get a kick out of their reactions to the decisions I tell them I would have made. They are human, although they seem to be spoken about as if they weren't sometimes. I also think that rules are made not to be broken, but overcome. For instance, I have asked many umpires for decisions on incidents that may never occur. Some occasionally do occur.

My favourite 'what if' question is, 'What if a batsman hits a ball flush into the middle stump at the bowler's end without the ball touching anything else, and it then ricochets back and knocks his bails off'. I get about half responding that he would be out, bowled, and the other half saying that he wouldn't be out as the stumps and the umpires are actually classified as part of the cricket field and not foreign objects, as some players think they are. The other 'what if' which tickles my fancy is to ask, 'When the batsmen have run two, and the umpire signals "one short", indicating that the striker has not completed his ground before turning for the second run, which one did he run short? The one coming up, or the one going back?' To this day, I haven't had one simple answer. I think they must both be short. However, the rules stick fast.

I also believe that the batter shouldn't attempt to run like the non-striker before the ball is delivered. If he advances he is attempting the equivalent of the non-striker backing up too far. I very carefully devised a tactic to stop Graham Yallop doing this against my bowling. I don't blame him, as I probably would have used similar tactics if I could have faced my own deliveries (which I almost can these days). I watched Graham for two matches as NSW played against Victoria in one-day limited over matches, and he advanced several yards down the wicket as I was approaching the crease. I practised my tactic in the nets in Tasmania prior to this particular game in Melbourne. I understood that the square-leg umpire would call me if I threw the ball and I got Steve Rixon, the NSW keeper to stand over the stumps and bring in a short-leg fieldsman (complete with helmet) then I would start my run. As soon as I saw the batsman heading down the wicket, I would prop, a couple of yards short of the crease, then throw the ball to the silly mid-on fielder, who would underarm it at the stumps. If he missed, Steve would be there to complete the run-out. In theory it sounded sensational.

I let both confidants know that I would try the plan on

Yallop's first attempt to advance, so they would need to be ready. He didn't keep us in suspense for long, as halfway through my first delivery he was charging down at a rate of knots. I could hardly believe my eyes, and neither could the other members of the NSW team who knew of my plan. I started to laugh halfway through my run up, but had to go through with it because the other two were waiting for me. My concentration wasn't what it should have been, and by this time I was actually laughing out aloud but I still propped and threw. My theory was that the umpire at square-leg should call me for throwing but since the batsman was attempting a run he should be run out. My aim was accurate enough.

Yallop backed towards the square-leg umpire and turned his back just as I threw and it hit him right in the middle of his back. The umpires conferred for two or three minutes before the umpire at the bowler's end called dead ball. Fortunately Graham's back was okay. He didn't come down the wicket again before I delivered the ball.

Coaches are a relatively new introduction to cricket. I don't particularly like the introduction of coaches at state and Australian level. For kids it is a different matter. I had my father who I always regarded as my coach. Many kids are the same these days. I still have great respect for fathers and some school-teachers who are prepared to put in extra hours after school. My main ambition as a kid was to play Test cricket for Australia. I often told my teachers that that was all I ever wanted to do, and homework for me was not necessary because I was only at school to fill in the years until I was old enough to play cricket for Australia. They told me every day that I would never achieve my ambition, and that I should conform like most of the other kids and concentrate on my school studies.

The schoolteachers I remember most are the late Jim Fuller,

John Gately, and Ray Johnson. I thank them. It isn't that they encouraged me to follow my dreams, but I think it often takes someone to tell you that you can't do something to bring out the determination in you. Jim Fuller wasn't one of the ones who said I didn't have a chance. He was actually the first teacher to play tennis and cricket with both me and the other kids. He believed that playing sport was a part of our education and we all thought he was great. He even stayed back after school to play these sports with us. It was a very small one-teacher school and we actually won a lot of sports carnivals and formed friendships that have lasted a lifetime. John and Ray were high-school teachers and both have retired in Dungog, my home town.

Coaching is very important for children and has a place right up until the first-class level when surely the players themselves become the best coaches. I enjoy coaching children. However, I don't think I could do it seven days a week, year in and year out. I coach during most school holidays and then I'm happy to see school go back. I find it is very satisfying to be able to show kids an easier way to do something. Good kids pick up these tips very quickly.

Cricket is really a simple game, although I feel that many so called 'experts' try to complicate it. I think that many coaching books are not done very well. Most say that the first thing a kid needs to learn is defence. I feel that most kids are too small to play defensive shots properly, especially back-foot ones. Children naturally like to hit the ball and score runs. I think they often know more than we do. The ball bounces too high for them to play with straight bats and they would be better off learning cross-batted shots first. If you watch a game involving children up to the under-14 age group you will notice that they score ninety percent of their runs behind the wicket by playing pull shots, hook shots and cuts, so why not assist these shots first? They do need to keep out some good balls, but it is a shame to waste the bad balls. Most fielding teams have only three players on the on-side, with the remainder on the offside, so obviously there must be more gaps on the on-side.

Both Mark and myself have been very good on-side players, so I guess that's why I find it annoying to see so many runs wasted as balls are bowled to the leg-side. That part of cricket hasn't changed, apart from behind square-leg where only two fielders are allowed. Even so, that's almost one quarter of the entire field so there still must be gaps to hit to in that area. I would prefer to see someone get out attacking rather than defending any day. So my advice to youngsters as well as seniors is that if the ball is there to be hit, then hit it.

On one occasion when we were in trouble during a Test match, Peter Burge told me that Sir Donald Bradman had advised him that the best option in such times was to always play your natural game. We were both attacking players and on this occasion both scored centuries, so it proved to be good advice.

There are two major changes that I have noticed with today's players which I don't really agree with. The first is the wearing of sunglasses while fielding. I have difficulty understanding why the players say they are so good for fielding, yet they don't wear them while they are batting. The second of these changes involves the acknowledgement to team-mates with the bat when they score 50 or 100. I always feel that the spectators should come first because the players rely on the support of the people who go to watch them and they should be acknowledged before team-mates. By waving their bats towards the dressing room, players appear to be suggesting that they have done it for the team, not to entertain the public, and I also feel that today's players do most things for themselves, not the team.

During my career I didn't encounter any reverse swing, as it's called these days. If I did encounter it, I don't think it had anything to do with the will of the bowler. I must say, I don't know whether there is such a thing. I actually feel that it is more a mistake made by the bowler. My theory is that all cricket balls weigh approximately five-and-half ounces although there is a slight leeway each side of this weight. The ball has a main seam around the centre, or close to the centre, and has six stitches, three on each side of the join in the two pieces of leather. Not all balls are actually identical and it is possible that one side of the ball could weigh slightly more than the other side. Bowlers have a preference for shining one side or the other of a ball. Some may choose to shine the brand side, while others would shine the reverse.

I maintain that the balls which swing in reverse are those in which the bowler has initially shone the 'lighter' side of the ball and, as he has continued, he has added sweat, eventually making this side heavier with moisture. I'm sure that the bowler would have swung the ball a lot more if he had chosen the 'heavier' side to begin with. I've actually placed new balls in a full glass of water to prove my point that one side is heavier than the other, but I guess a bowler really doesn't care a great deal as long as he is doing something with the ball.

I can remember a story involving changes to the game which begins with an occasion when I was invited to the home of Sir Donald and Lady Bradman for morning tea. It was shortly after my retirement from first-class cricket, and I was in Adelaide working on match commentary. The English team had also been invited and it was at a time when they were struggling to handle the West Indies' barrage of pace bowlers (like every other team in the world at that stage). A few of the English players were questioning Sir Donald on how he thought he would handle these fast bowlers if he had been facing them these days. They also asked whether he would score as many runs. I was fascinated by Sir Donald's reply.

He said a lot of things had changed since he played cricket and he went on to outline some of the changes. His first point surprised me, as he said that the wickets were nowhere near as good these days as they had been when he was playing. He then went on to say that the field restrictions on the leg-side had made a big difference because unlimited men were allowed behind square-leg in his day. He added that the captains do a lot more homework on the game, and the bowlers bowl to a plan which is better nowadays. I was watching a few of the Englishmen and could see that they were smiling because they were thinking they had nailed the great man.

Then Sir Donald went on to say, 'In answer to your question, no, I wouldn't have scored as many runs today as I did in my time, but I would still have scored a lot more than the fellow that comes second.' The facial expressions changed very quickly as they were left without an argument. I don't think anyone could dispute that Sir Donald was absolutely right.

I think overall the majority of changes to the game of cricket have been for the better. I also feel that it is going to be important to keep the umpires out in the middle in the future, even with the third umpire and camera assistance. They have a special part to play on the ground as well.

CHARACTER LOST TO PROFESSIONALISM

'This change to the match referee's scope has, in my opinion, taken something away from the aggression and excitement of the game.'

There have been a great many changes made to the game both on and off the field since I have been playing, and since Doug was playing. The game must inevitably change with the times and the developing technology. I would say, however, that by far the biggest change is the introduction of the third umpire on run-outs and stumpings. It is a change that I welcome.

Over the years, there have surely been hundreds of instances when players have been run out but they haven't been given out because it was humanly impossible to decide. The third umpire picks up things that no one would have picked up no matter how closely they were watching. It is, of course, much harder

155

on the batsmen. No one gets away with what they used to get away with, whether intentional or not. There's no more getting away with a close run-out because the umpire isn't sure. Now they call for the third umpire and, in an instant, the decision is made. Occasionally, of course, it could have worked the other way in the past, when batsmen were out but given in.

The third umpire has made an enormous difference. In a small way it has also made the game a little slower and a little less spontaneous for those watching. On the other hand, it has also created more tension when there's a close call and the game is hanging in the balance. Everyone looks up at the lights. Will it be red or green? Other times the umpires are calling for the third umpire when it isn't close at all just to make absolutely sure. That holds the game up. There is no doubt that the third umpire can decide a game, especially in the one-day matches.

Sometimes in the past the keeper may have hit the stump with his hands—perhaps accidentally—but you'd never get away with such action now. I like the third umpire because it minimises the umpires' mistakes. I think it will eventually be brought in for LBW rulings as well although I'm not sure how they'll manage that. I believe that if there is any way you can eliminate mistakes then that can only be good for the game. Other sports, like rugby league, tennis and horseracing, all use electronic or technical devices to help the process of decision making.

The bumper or bouncer ruling in the past was limited to six balls per over instead of the two we're allowed today. Sometimes a bowler would bowl a bouncer for every ball in an innings if that's what he wanted to do. To me that was terribly boring and defeats the purpose of the game. If you couldn't hook, you couldn't make a run. If you couldn't hit the ball, it took a lot of shots away from the game, and I don't think it gave the crowd value for money. It was dull. People don't want to watch bouncers all day. I think the ruling of two per innings is a welcome rule change. Two bouncers is a good number. You can still intimidate the batsman or get him out hooking. The bouncer is a big weapon for a fast bowler because it scares batsmen and that makes them easier to deal with. If you make it any less than two per over you are denying the bowler an integral part of his repertoire.

The no-ball rule is a significant change to the game. Changing from the back foot to the front foot and having to be behind the popping crease makes it a little easier for the batsmen. Gone are the days of bowlers being able to have a big drag in their bowling stride in order to gain that extra yard or so. There is no room for error now. If you're on the line it's a no-ball.

The bowlers, of course, used to be able to bowl and then leave the field for a rest. I think that was unfair to the batsmen who had to stay out there. The new rule, that unless you're badly injured you have to have permission from the umpire to leave the field, is also a positive change.

As we know, if you're off the field for 15 minutes, every minute beyond that adds to the length of time it will take before you're allowed to bowl again. I think it is fair that the bowlers now have to stay out there and do the hard work along with the batsmen. They did used to bowl eight balls per over and now it's six which evens it up a bit in the bowlers' favour. Six balls only means the bowler doesn't tire as quickly, as they are working in shorter bursts.

The covered pitch is of course relatively new. I suspect in Doug's day they would often, or almost always, play on uncovered pitches. That was difficult for the batsmen as they were playing on wet, sticky wickets. Nowadays, all first-class cricket and all Test matches are played on covered pitches. At the end of the day or when it rains the pitch is covered. Once again this is one for the batsmen over the bowlers. Bowlers like Derek Underwood bowling fast spinners would have been impossible to bat against and it would have been quite dangerous facing Allan Donald. I'll take covered pitches any day.

The role of the match referees is a big change to the game. They have become far more prominent with all the cameras that are now focused on the players. We have to be so much more careful about our code of conduct. You can't even swear now without it being picked up. I'm not saying for a minute this is a bad thing but simply that the surveillance and fining of players for on-field misbehaviour has become much more intense in recent years.

This change to the match referee's scope has, in my opinion, taken something away from the aggression and excitement of the game. The natural confrontations between batsman and bowler have become so subdued to be almost nonexistent. You can't even show any level of annoyance over a bad decision anymore. If you're incorrectly given out LBW for getting an inside edge onto your pad, for example, you can't show your bat to the umpire or you may well be fined. You have to just walk and show no emotion.

I'm in no way suggesting that we should be disputing every decision, but I believe this intense scrutiny and threat of fines for minor misdemeanours is making the players more robotic and a whole lot less flamboyant. You can't show much human expression or natural feeling. People do love to watch that edgy confrontation between batsman and bowler, but these days the match referee is pretty strict about stamping that behaviour out. I do think the severity of the scrutiny takes something away from the game. I'm a pretty quiet player anyway, but people like Merv Hughes used to be very entertaining. Everyone used to love watching Merv bowl and stir up the batsman. All that huff and puff used to be great and, as far as I can see, hardly detrimental to the game. Glenn McGrath has probably been the latest to suffer from the eagle eye of the camera. He was fined for spitting, something which would never have been picked up in days gone by.

I must reiterate that I'm not suggesting we all go out and

behave like idiots or that we would want to. It wouldn't be like that anyway. A player's natural character could come through— some are quiet and some more emotional. I think a lot of the characters are now lost to the game. What is wrong with a bit of emotion? It's all part of life, and I'm not so sure that the kids shouldn't see a bit of banter on the field from time to time.

Another positive change, however, is the introduction of the neutral umpires. We now have a local and overseas umpire at every Test match regardless of where we are. They definitely needed to make that change. If you have two local umpires, they will be under pressure from the home side and the home crowd. I'm not saying that anyone cheats, but the perception was there that they could. This new structure, with the neutral umpire, rules out the possibility of that negative perception. The International Cricket Council (ICC) realised it was required, and I applaud the move.

A seemingly minor change, but one which I also support, is the turning on of lights at Test matches. Once again, I think this is good because it gives the crowds value for money. Why shouldn't they see as much cricket as possible? Of course it doesn't follow that both teams will automatically agree to use the lights and it takes the agreement of both teams before the lights are switched on. During one match in 1998, England said no to the lights. They obviously thought that they had less chance of winning than we did if we stayed out there, so they voted not to switch the lights on which ended the day's play. I think it should be a hard and fast rule that if the lights are required and they are available they should be switched on. The crowds are there to see us play and that's exactly what we should do. More cricket equals more results equals more entertainment.

There have been several changes to cricket equipment and apparel. Heavier bats are used by players today. Sachin Tendulkar, for example, uses a bat which is well over 3 pounds

(1.4 kilograms). Helmets are a big change from Doug's era. We all wear them now and wouldn't think about going out there without a helmet. I've seen footage from Doug's era where the players are fielding right up close to the batsman without helmets. I would never do that for fear of being killed, especially on the leg-side. They're still not compulsory but I can't think of a single player since Viv Richards who didn't wear a helmet in first-class cricket. It used to be a bit of a macho thing not to wear a helmet and all the little kids used to refuse to wear them because they thought it was sissy. Now it's just a matter of common sense and most people at all levels wear helmets. It's just a basic fact that if you get seriously injured and you're put out of the side for a few months you may never get back in. Nearly every side has at least two fast bowlers all wanting to get you out and perhaps knock your head off!

Sunglasses are an additional part of the players' kit these days and I know my good friend Doug doesn't agree with their use on the field. I, on the other hand, think they're a great idea for the fieldsmen. Instead of squinting for six hours on a sunny day, or even a cloudy day when it's still quite glary, your eyes can be totally relaxed. The sunglasses also help prevent dust and wind irritating the eyes, which can be a real problem on the subcontinent. Some players wear them to bat as well, like Brian Lara and Jack Russell, to mention a couple. I find that wearing them to bat doesn't quite work because of the sweat that builds up inside your helmet and drips down the lenses. It isn't conducive to a clear view. Maybe Bollé could invent a pair with windscreen wipers?

I do think that it was a lot less pressured when Doug played the game. He might argue differently, but I think it is the case in most sports that a lot of the character and feeling has gone from the game at the top level. We're so conscious of image now that it is slightly unreal. I think that's a shame. Still, cricket is drawing very good crowds in this country so I guess people are still enjoying the spectacle. I'm not knocking the spectacle but just acknowledging the changes.

We do feel that whatever we do we're under a microscope a lot of the time. We're aware of the image we're supposed to project, and I accept that's part of what is required. When I started at Test level nine years ago we didn't have such intense media pressure. We also didn't have such a tight and carefully run infrastructure around us.

We now have a team psychologist, a nutritionist, a fitness trainer, a physio, a coach, a media officer and a full-time manager. Now they leave nothing to chance. When I first started, we had a physio, a coach and a part-time manager. Even all our food is selected for us by a dietitian.

A lot more is expected of the players. We used to sit down after a game and have a beer and a chat. Now after a day's play you have to go out and stretch on the ground. We do a warm down and then a swim at the hotel. We're not supposed to drink alcohol until an hour after the game to rehydrate. We've all got tailored fitness programs which the trainer prepares.

As far as fitness goes, you're expected to work at it. All of this is supposed to make us last longer with fewer injuries. The idea is you stay fitter through the whole season. You're supposed to drink less alcohol and eat properly. I don't think we get fewer injuries than before, but the fact is we also play a lot more cricket now so it's hard to compare.

South Africa are back in the competition and Sri Lanka are playing a lot more. There are simply more teams and more competitions to play. We're touring so much more. There are all these extra one-day tournaments like those in Bangladesh, Sharjah and at the Commonwealth Games. Zimbabwe, too, are a new side on the international fixture list. So there is a lot of cricket being played and a lot more time away from home.

I don't enjoy playing quite as much as I used to because of the number of games we're playing. There is a burn-out level. For example, seven one-day games in a row against the same team does get a bit much. We're playing every week and training constantly in between. I'm not saying any of us has reached that level and I think our cricket shows that we haven't, but they have to be careful that they don't push too hard because players will, at the least, get injured if they're overplaying.

Overall, I think the majority of changes have been positive and that the game is heading in the right direction but, as I have said, we have also changed the character of the game to a certain extent.

CHAPTER TEN

THE CHARACTERS

THEY DON'T MAKE THEM LIKE THEY USED TO

'There was never a dull moment when Ashley was around.
He once stood on his own spinning finger while he was
wearing spiked boots.'

I think that cricket tends to produce great characters. Perhaps this is because it can take up to five days to complete a match, but whatever the reason, more funny stories about great characters seem to come out of cricket than out of other sports. I never played against Fred Trueman in a Test match but we have been in opposing teams when we have been fundraising for different charities. Most people tell me that Fred was the funniest man of all to have played cricket for his country, and I have been in his company socially and found that I enjoyed the experience.

Many Fred Trueman stories are legendary. The first one that

I recall concerned the Reverend David Sheppard. David was never known for his great fielding, and on one particular occasion when he was playing in a team with Fred he had dropped several catches and let a few balls past him on the field as well. When yet another ball went straight between his legs for four off Freddie's bowling, it was clear that things were not going at all well for either David or Fred. At the end of Fred's over, the Reverend walked up to Fred and apologized to him. He said, 'Sorry Fred, I should have kept my legs together'. Fred quickly snapped back an angry reply, 'Not thee lad, thy bloody mother'.

On another occasion when I was in Kingston, Jamaica, playing in a benefit game for Sir Garfield Sobers, I was at a bar with Fred and another great fast bowler, Wesley Hall. As usual, Fred was leading the conversation and he directed his attention to Wes.

'Wes, I wish I could have bowled as fast as you. I reckon I would have been unplayable if I had.'

'Man,' Wes replied, 'you didn't have to bowl as fast as me because you swung the ball both ways in the air, and it seamed off the wicket. You captured over 300 Test wickets Fred, you didn't do too badly in your career.'

'I suppose you're right,' Fred said. 'But if I could have bowled at your pace, I would have got a lot more.'

During this whole conversation, Fred's language was much more colourful, as he had added many of his infamous unprintable adjectives. Anyway, this conversation went back and forth for about 40 minutes, when Fred added another twist to it. He said, 'I suppose you're right, Wes. You know, every ball I bowled during my entire career did something. It either swung in, or swung away, or seamed in, or seamed away. That is, all except for one.'

Well, Wes thought this was going a bit overboard. He said, 'Fred, I agree that you were a great bowler, but I don't think you can honestly say that every ball you bowled, except one, did something! I'm sorry, I can't agree with that.'

As quick as a wink, Fred then replied, 'Come to think of it Wes, you know, even that bugger might have done just a little bit'.

By this stage, everyone around the bar had joined in to listen, and the whole bar just erupted in laughter. Fred is one of the few characters that I have come across who could get away with colourful language in all company. He didn't ever have a conversation without swearing.

The late Johnny Martin is another character who comes readily to my mind. He was a left-handed orthodox spin bowler. He always provided us with plenty of laughs. Johnny was always known as the 'Favourite' or the 'Little Fave'. He came from Burrell Creek in the Taree area of NSW. This isn't too far from my home town of Dungog. John caught the train down from Taree every weekend for grade, Shield, and even Test matches. He could name all the train stations between Taree and Sydney's Central Station, both forwards and in reverse. John also knew whether his train stopped at each station or whether it didn't. He was a person who was loved by everyone who met him.

People from the country never seem to have enough rain, and often when John was asked how things were going in Taree, he would say, 'It's so dry, you could flog a flea all around the paddocks without losing him'. That is dry. Of course people were also curious as to why John would choose to live in the country and spend so much time travelling to Sydney to play cricket, and they would ask him what he did up there in Burrell Creek. John usually explained that his family manned the local telephone exchange which was a party line. I was probably the only one who knew about a party line because we'd had one at one stage when I lived in the country. Our number was Marshdale I.U. and two other farms on the party line shared this number. We knew the call was for us if it rang two shorts and a long. Others might have two longs and a short, and so on. Often all three parties would have a three-way conversation.

Apart from manning this exchange, John had a few acres of land where he kept some cattle and horses. He was also frequently asked how the cattle and horses got on, seeing it was so dry. John would reply, 'The cattle aren't so bad, we feed them hay'. Of course this didn't explain how the horses got on. The next question would be, 'What about the horses, don't they eat hay?' 'Oh, yes they do,' he'd say. 'But we had to get rid of the black horses. You see, we had a lot of black horses, and a lot of white horses.' Well by this time, he had people really intrigued and of course they couldn't help asking the next question. 'Why did you sell all the black horses?' Answer from John, 'The black horses ate more hay than the white horses'. You can just imagine how interested everyone would be by this time, trying to figure out how the horses' colour could influence how much they ate, and they'd asked John right on cue. 'How come black horses eat more than white horses?' With a perfectly straight face, John would answer, 'We had far more black horses than white horses'. I felt that both Fred and John could have made a living on stage as comedians— they were great entertainers, both on and off the cricket field.

Another different character who was hilariously funny was Ashley Mallett. Ashley never meant to be funny but it was often said he was an accident waiting to happen. He was very clumsy and he had poor eyesight. To walk from one side of the room to the other he could actually knock tables over, and this didn't involve any alcoholic drinks he was known to enjoy. It was just amazing that, despite his clumsiness, Ashley took some incredible catches. He must have always worn his contact lenses onto the field to do this. I can remember numerous times when he lost them, and we, his mates, were always a wonderful help, stamping around to help him find them.

Ashley has a great fear of snakes, spiders, crawling insects and most other small bugs that move. When I played cricket with him I witnessed some incredible reactions if little foreign bodies landed on him, and I loved to play tricks with fake spiders and snakes just to watch his reaction. He frequently spilled things on other people's clothes and bags so I needed to exercise some caution at times. Other team members often helped. Several times we put witches' wool in the ashtray. We didn't have to wait long for Ashley to find it, but, more often than not, the full ashtray ended up in someone else's bag. We always had plenty of cigarettes in my playing days—I worked for Rothmans, and Benson & Hedges were the main sponsors of the Australian team. Packets of cigarettes were always lying about on tables everywhere we went. I loved to visit trick shops whenever we toured and check out all the gimmicks that were available. Poor Ashley was always my prime target.

At one trick shop I found some small caps that you could push into the tobacco, and I put a couple into the cigarettes of an open packet that was lying on the table. Ashley didn't keep us waiting for too long. As luck would have it, he lit a loaded cigarette and after a couple of puffs the cigarette exploded on cue. It ended up burning a hole in someone's shirt after he threw it away. This trick was worth repeating and I got good mileage out of it.

There was never a dull moment when Ashley was around. He once stood on his own spinning finger while he was wearing spiked boots. This put him out of action just when we could have used him because the pitch was turning.

Max Walker had a reputation for being a character in my time. I would class Max as more of a raconteur. He has a great imagination, and he said once that his father told him not to let the truth get in the way of a good story. I am sure he follows that lesson. Maxie is never short of a story and he tells some very good ones. I sometimes wonder where I was when they happened because I am often the main character in them. Max always has a smile on his face. He earned the nickname of 'Tangles' or 'Tangle-foot' because of his unusual bowling action and he almost appeared to lack coordination, I think because of his size. Max is a big guy and once he got his body moving, he found it hard to stop. You never got in his way if he was going for a catch. I can understand why he was a good Aussie Rules player.

Merv Hughes appeared similar to Max in stature and was a more recent character of the game. Mark probably knows many more stories about Merv than I do, but I did hear once that Bob Simpson, who was the Australian coach when Merv was playing Test cricket, banned the players from drinking, apart from those they had in the dressing room after each day's play. Merv apparently wanted to move his bed into the dressing room.

Now that Merv has semi-retired from first-class cricket, I wonder how big he will grow. He's like me in that he doesn't enjoy running very much, and he also appears to like his food.

Cricket today doesn't seem to produce as many players who are a bit out of the ordinary. The spectators often look for alternative entertainment when there is a lull in play. I liked the way the crowds reacted to Merv when he was playing, and he also took the crowd taunts with good humour, which is all they want. It doesn't hurt to acknowledge the crowd and show that you can take the bad as well as the good. Within reason, the odd sip from a can over the fence (providing the person offering it looks friendly), is not out of hand. I do advise caution with this practice, however, because some players have ended up with weird tastes in their mouths at times.

The West Indian crowds love players to acknowledge them. They understand cricket very well, but if things slow down on the field, they look for something else to entertain them. Many people in the crowd are very witty, and you can hear some funny things being shouted when you're out in the middle.

I have been told that Keith Miller was a jester as well. The record books have shown me that he was one of the world's greatest all-rounders. I played in a benefit match for Keith and Ray Lindwall who was a superb opening bowler during his era. The match was at Manly Oval and I think Keith was on time for the start of play on this occasion, although it wouldn't have mattered if he had been late. Keith captained NSW for a time, and apparently he wasn't always there in time to toss the coin at the start of play.

Peter Philpott was recalling one of his early games for NSW one day, and he said that Keith was supposed to pick him up at North Sydney on his way to the SCG. Peter was like all players playing their first matches at a higher level, and he didn't sleep very well. He didn't want to be late and was ready and waiting on time. Well, while Peter didn't sleep very well, Keith didn't sleep at all. His wife had just given birth, and Keith had celebrated this big event right through the night and morning. He was running very late to pick up young Philpott at North Sydney. Peter, in the meantime, was anxiously trying to think of other ways to get to the SCG. He finally settled down and decided that he might as well wait for his captain, as surely this was a pretty fair excuse for running late.

Finally Keith turned up to collect Peter, and they arrived at the ground with only minutes to spare before the start of play. South Australia were batting and Keith had only half completed his change into cricket gear when the umpires came to start play for the day. The NSW team huddled in a bunch in the centre of the ground waiting for field placement, but at this stage they didn't even know who would open the attack. Someone apparently asked Keith where they should go and he just said, 'Scatter'.

Of course the wicket-keeper had a fair idea where he should be, but none of the others were too sure. After scattering, someone else asked Keith who was going to bowl. He said, 'Oh, give me the bloody ball and I'll do that'. The record book states that he took 7 wickets for 12 runs and South Australia were bowled out for 27. The night on the town apparently didn't hurt Keith.

Keith Miller had an excellent memory for people's names. He not only remembered both first and surnames, but where and when he met people. I believe there was only one occasion when he made an error. This was in a country town at a Lord Mayoral reception, and Keith was responding to the Mayor's speech. He thanked the local council for the hospitality that had been given to the players, and made all the other points required in such a speech. Keith finished the speech by saying, 'It has been great to be here in this town, whatever it's bloody well called'. I'm sure he never made the same mistake with that town again.

I do know that his memory doesn't usually let him down in this way because I have been with Keith when he has walked up to people that he hasn't seen for 20 or 30 years and made himself known to them. He would help them recall things like, 'It was in 1942, on the tenth of January, at such and such a place'. I know this was during the war, but the war lasted for six years, so he must have met a lot of people in that time. Keith was a pilot during World War II. The people he was renewing acquaintances with were his fellow servicemen from those years, and they were as surprised as I was at the time.

Many people recognize Keith Miller because of his wonderful talent on the cricket field, but it's incredible to see his memory for other people as well. I hold in awe people with this ability. I'm sure that Keith and I would have got on very well if we had played cricket at the same time.

Cricket has changed a great deal since the days of Keith Miller and since my days, for that matter. I doubt that we would have gotten away with nearly as much if we were playing today. Keith has been known to duck off from the SCG to take in a couple of races at Randwick while his side was batting. Once during a Test match in Sydney, Greg Chappell and I suggested to Ian Chappell that if this was good enough for Keith Miller, then we should be able to do it too. The suggestion came about after we saw the opening bowler from Pakistan deliver the first ball at very medium pace. Greg and I looked at each other and thought that there was no way either of us was going to get a bat that day. Greg was batting at number four and I was after him. Ian wasn't at all amused by us taking the opposition so lightly and sternly reprimanded us for the joke. I think we were both batting before lunch as it turned out, so I'm not sure how Keith managed it.

Ian wasn't one for taking any opposition lightly, whether it was on the cricket field or the billiard table. He was, and still is, a very competitive man. For a long time he refused to play tennis against his first wife as she was a top player and could always beat him. These days, after many lessons, he is a top-class tennis player himself. He is even enjoying tennis more than the golf that he always loved to play whenever we had a day off during cricket tours.

Brian Taber and I challenged Ian and Graeme Watson to a game of golf about 15 years ago, but it has been continually postponed because we can't agree on Ian's handicap. Three of us have official handicaps but Ian doesn't anymore. He played with a single-figure handicap when he was keen and playing regularly, but we can't accept that it could be in the twenties now. However, that's Ian—he still hates to lose.

Anyway, with the way Brian and I are playing at the moment, we will both soon have official handicaps in the twenties so we could spend the next 15 years trying to convince Ian that he should take us up on the challenge.

THE SPINNERS

'Just as he looked up, with absolute perfect timing,
he caught the ball on his face.'

In my career I've been fortunate enough to meet a lot of interesting people. Among them there have also been some unusual
but fantastic characters. I have found that many of those characters are the spin and fast bowlers. For some reason they are
always the standout members of the team, perhaps because it is
a role that requires confidence and flair.

Probably one of the most outstanding amongst everybody is
Merv Hughes—the lovable larrikin. He is easily the most memorable character I have ever played with. Merv is larger than life
with that big moustache, big heart and big appetite. Amongst
his team-mates he was known as the fruit fly, the great
Australian pest.

Merv never seemed to be quiet while in the dressing room or

175

while on tour. He was always throwing things around the room, telling jokes and generally getting in the way. At times you'd wish he'd just quieten down a little, but on tours when there was little to do or when the team wasn't going so well he was the one who livened things up, made us laugh and put a smile on your face.

On my Test debut against England in Adelaide, Merv was my first roomie. I'm not sure whether this was because no one would put up with him, so he was given to the unsuspecting rookie, or because they thought he'd help the new boy on the block relax in his first Test. Anyway, it was quite good fun sharing with him, despite his tendency to order room service at any hour of the day to satisfy his ever-present hunger pains. Then there was the early morning wake-up call of the big man jumping on your head and yelling in your ear.

I remember a time when our fitness trainer and physio, Errol Alcott, was weighing all the players and doing fat ratio tests on us. Merv was the next one up, and all the boys in the team were eager to watch him complete his test to see what would happen. First of all there were the calipers to measure fat on seven or eight parts of the body. Merv went straight to the top of the class. Next, Errol asked Merv to jump on the scales to be weighed. Merv responded with 'I beg your pardon?' Errol was annoyed and said, 'Stop mucking around. Just jump on the scales.' Merv obliged and did exactly as Errol asked. He literally jumped onto the scales and smashed them completely. Errol was disgusted but the rest of us were happy to see the scales had been dismantled so efficiently.

Merv wasn't just a great cricketer to know off the field. He was great on the field as well. In South Africa in 1994, Merv had problems with a back injury, and his first game after being out injured was a warm-up match against Orange Free State before the first Test. It was to be used by us as a fitness test to see how Merv was going. Everybody was watching with interest to see what would happen.

At the beginning of Orange Free State's first innings Mark Taylor handed Merv the ball for a bowl. Halfway through his first over after lunch, Merv pulled up and crouched over, part of the way down the wicket, after bowling the third ball of the over. We all thought the worst had happened and he looked to be really suffering. We all thought his back injury had reoccurred and was even more serious this time. Mark Taylor was obviously very worried about his prized fast bowler and immediately ran to Merv's aid. Merv was still bent over and he looked up at Mark Taylor and let rip with an almighty fart and then said, 'No problem. Fit as a fiddle,' and proceeded to bowl.

Merv could be annoying but ultimately he was a great team man, a great competitor and a great bowler. I liked having him in the team. He was definitely one of the last great characters.

For some reason, spin bowlers are always different from the rest of the team. Greg Matthews was no exception to that rule. Greg, with his different hair, different language and different clothes—he always wore bandannas, jeans with stripes and loud shirts—really stood out from the pack.

Everything with Greg was 'How ya going, man?' 'Yeah, man.' 'Cool, man.' He speaks a different language to the rest of the guys. As most people know, he's with Advanced Hair Studio and he's very preoccupied about the appearance of his new hair. I know some people might think this is rich coming from me because I have a reputation for worrying about the neatness of my hair, but I'm nothing compared to Greg.

He's getting paid big money by Advanced Hair to look good and he certainly isn't shy with the hairdo. He's a confident sort of guy anyway. Every time we have drinks, he gets the twelfth man to bring out a comb or a brush. He gets a glass of water and throws it over his head and brushes his hair in front of everybody. He swings it around and rubs his hands through it.

He couldn't care less what we all think or what anyone thinks. I'd say he'd be the first player to brush his hair on the field like this. They say I like brushing my hair but I've never done it on the field.

When Stephen and I made that big partnership of 464 against Western Australia in Perth, Greg said to us that if we were not out at stumps on the first day, wherever we went for dinner he'd wear his cricket pads.

With that sort of incentive Stephen and I played the best innings of our lives and we were 100-odd not out overnight. By the time we declared the next afternoon I think I had made 229 and Stephen made 216. Greg remained true to his word and wore his pads out through the streets of an exclusive Perth suburb and into a classy restaurant. He had his nice silk shirt, his trendy purple jeans and his cricket pads. He just walked through the streets wearing the pads wherever we went. Everyone was staring but that was obviously what he wanted. He likes to be noticed.

Tim May is another spinner who comes to mind as a character. I guess many people wouldn't think of Tim as a character but he has a very dry sense of humour—almost arid—and he likes picking on himself. All his humour is self deprecating and he never has a positive word to say on his own behalf. This is strange in a Test side. Most guys, if not all, who play for Australia are usually very confident in their own ability and like to brag about themselves in different ways. Tim is the opposite. He's one of those athletes who doesn't have a lot of natural ability and not a lot of coordination. He tells us about his life as a child when he broke his arm 15 times. He tells us that this is absolutely true. Some of his broken-arm stories have him trying to jump the tennis court nets at the end of a game and falling over and breaking his arm; he fell off bikes and out of trees; and like the rest of us, also hurt himself playing football.

He's the type of guy that, if anyone is going to get injured, it will be him. He's unlucky and almost seems to will the bad luck on himself. I remember there was a training session on the Ashes tour in 1989. I wasn't there but someone told me the story of when the guys were training at Lord's. It was May in England and very cold. At one end of the field were the nets where you bat and bowl, and at the other end, about 100 metres away, some guys were having catching practice. You'd think you'd be pretty safe down there but as it turns out, Tim was doing some short-catching practice when the cry went up, 'Look out!' Tom Moody had hit a tracer ball of a drive out of the nets. Then someone yelled out 'Look out, Tim!', and he did.

Just as he looked up, the ball skidded off the turf and hit him straight in the mouth knocking some of his teeth out. He had stitches and the works. It could only happen to Tim May. With absolutely perfect timing, he caught the ball on his face. He is born unlucky in the injury department.

He often makes fun of his batting prowess. He's always saying he can't bat, or bowl or field for that matter. I do remember him hitting me for six in a Mercantile Mutual Cup game in Adelaide, so it is clearly untrue. Fielding is something he hates doing. He doesn't have confidence in his own ability to catch and throw the ball accurately. He tells us he's dropped ten caught-and-bowled catches in a row. This would have to be something of a record.

I remember another story from Lord's in 1993, when Tim was fielding at fine-leg and Graham Gooch was batting. Merv was bowling and he bowled a bouncer. Gooch hooked and he got a top edge. The ball flew down to fine-leg and Tim May. Tim had to run a good 15 or 20 metres to get to the ball. He scampered around the boundary and dived full length. He dived into the turf and there was grass and mud flying everywhere. Heaven forbid, he caught the ball. We all ran down to him and said 'Great catch', 'Good on you', 'Well done', 'Unbelievable'. He was sort of stunned and he got up and said 'What happened? Who did I catch? Who's out?' Tim was in a world of his own when he caught that ball. I always think of him as very dry, telling a lot of jokes but generally not saying a lot. He is just very funny in his own quiet way.

Shane Warne, yet another spin bowler, is a very funny character too, but he's loud with a capital 'L'. Like Merv he is larger than life and a complete individual. He's the Elvis Presley of Australian cricket. Everywhere he goes people love him or hate him. He's always the centre of attention and he stands out for being different. He always drives flash cars and he wears less than conservative clothes, with the earring and his hair dyed blonde. He doesn't care what people think about him.

I first met him after a day's play in a Sheffield Shield match between NSW and Victoria in Sydney. He had only played a couple of games but had gotten a big wrap after a successful Australian XI tour of Zimbabwe. However, with his portly figure, cigarette in his mouth and cheeky facial features, he looked more like John Daly, the American golfer, than an Australian cricketer. He looked anything but an Australian superstar. How times have changed since then, especially after a very slow start to his Test career. In my opinion he has been the best known and most popular Australian cricketer, and maybe even sportsman, since Sir Donald Bradman.

Warnie wouldn't look out of place wandering down Sunset Boulevard or Rodeo Drive with those movie-star looks. Blond hair, green eyes, pearly white teeth. All are instantly recognized by cricket spectators worldwide. Rooming with him is hard work. You feel like a receptionist or private secretary answering phone calls from fans every two seconds.

Shane is much sought after in the corporate world, being the face of big companies like Nike, Just Jeans and so on. He has been on the catwalk with Helena Christensen and there is a wax model likeness of him at Madame Tussaud's, so you can see he is somewhat different to the average Test or first-class cricketer. Behind that face, however, is a cricketer who fits into the team very well. He gives out a bit of stick and cops a bit of stick.

Warnie's eating habits are the strangest of any human being's I've ever encountered. His staple diet consists of toasted cheese sandwiches, chips, Twisties, margherita pizzas, spaghetti, and Four 'n' Twenty pies. That's it. No salads, no vegetables, no chicken, no seafood, no fruit. Nothing a nutritionist would recommend. That is it. I don't know where he finds the energy to bowl 50 overs in 40-degree heat. It is a mystery, and certainly a minor miracle, that he can do it. He must be like a car with the petrol gauge continually on the reserve tank but still managing to chug along. We've been to Doyle's Seafood Restaurant in Sydney and Warnie ate a bread roll. After many a team function at the very best restaurants, Warnie has ordered in a takeaway pizza because he won't eat anything on the menu. Each to their own, I guess, and it certainly hasn't done his bowling any harm.

Around the dressing room he's a bit of a character. Impersonations are a specialty and favourite pastime. He can go through our whole batting order and take off all the different styles down to a T. The Steve Waugh cut shot or the Mark Waugh flick off the pads are some of his best and present no problem for the seasoned performer. He can also do past players like Dean Jones, Merv Hughes and Ian Chappell. Shane's Ian Chappell is particularly good, with the collar up, the chewing gum, fiddling with his box and taking the classic hook shot.

Warnie is also really good with the voice impersonations and he can mimic the Channel 9 commentary team brilliantly.

I remember a particularly dull Test match function in Perth one year when Shane was to be interviewed by Bill Lawry on stage. Instead of the usual question-and-answer session, that are the standard fare at such functions, Shane answered the questions in a mixture of Bill Lawry and Tony Greig dulcet tones. He certainly livened things up as he always does. Ultimately, though, I think of Shane Warne as the greatest spinner of all time, a classic character, and a pleasure to have as a team-mate.

All these characters I've described have made me and the other players laugh, which is a great ability to have in life. When you're away touring and under pressure, these are the sort of players who help keep things in perspective and also make the social life more enjoyable. After all, they say laughter is the best medicine.

A time when everyone was still itching to bowl, or keep wicket, or bat, yet when there was no immediate call to do any of these, and most of the usual social contacts were absent, they too found something much more congenial than, say, a gathering of railway directors might do in similar circumstances. The pictures and the broken things in the drawing room show what they did with it.

CHAPTER ELEVEN

FAVOURITE FUNNY STORIES

THE CASE OF THE
REVERENT UMPIRE

'We called John "Cho" for "Cricket Hours Only".
We didn't see a lot of him off the field.'

Nearly all cricketers play golf for a number of different reasons. I don't play as well as Mark. I'm off a very moderate handicap of seventeen. I'm actually pleased I never chose to play golf seriously. I often tell the story about a pretty ordinary golfer, who could even be described as the worst golfer in the world. He used to hook, slice, shank, take air swings—in fact, he had developed every bad habit a golfer could develop. Finally, he was going so badly that a group of friends agreed to put in enough money to send him to the club professional for some lessons.

This particular golfer went to the pro every day for a fortnight, but his golf continued to get worse. The pro was about to despair, and when the world's worst golfer walked in for yet another lesson, on this particular day he said, 'Look, you're wasting my time and your money! I have given you a golf lesson every day for the past two weeks, and your golf has actually got worse! I can't believe you're hooking and slicing even more than you were before you came. Your golf is just shot to ribbons, in fact you're hopeless!'

Well the poor golfer felt pretty disillusioned by this tirade, but persisted in asking for help. The professional relented. He said, 'Oh well, you see, golf is a confidence game. Perhaps it will help your confidence if you go out and play 18 holes without a ball. Go through the whole exercise. Put your tee in the ground, imagine that there's a ball on it, get your driver out of your bag, and just imagine that you've hit it straight down the fairway. Chase after it, get your iron out, and just imagine that you've put it up on the green. Get up on the green, get your putter out of your bag, and imagine that you have put it in the hole. Eighteen holes will fix you,' he said.

This fellow was going so badly that he thought he might as well give this suggestion a try. The following afternoon, he wandered onto the first tee. He had a good look around, to make sure that nobody was watching, and put his tee into the ground. Next he reached for his driver and was halfway through his backswing, when another fellow jumped out of the bushes, right behind him. 'Hey,' the stranger yelled, 'you haven't put a ball on the tee.' Well the world's worst golfer had to tell him the sad story about the professional's advice. 'That's funny,' replied the stranger, 'he told me exactly the same thing.'

Between them, they decided that they might as well play the 18 holes together, and the stranger went to his car to get his clubs out of the boot. When he returned, he said, 'Well, you've got your tee in the ground, you might as well hit off first'. Anyway, he was halfway through his backswing, when again, the stranger interrupted.

'Wait a minute,' the stranger said. 'When I play golf, I normally have a bit of a side bet. Are you interested in that?'

'Oh yes,' the world's worst golfer replied. 'I normally play for a few dollars myself. How about we make it five, five, ten?' His 'opponent' agreed and the round commenced.

The stranger was standing right behind our friend the world's worst golfer, adding his comments. 'Gee, you've struck that well,' he said. 'Straight as a dart, over the fairway bunker, right down the middle. Great shot, about 240 metres, I'd say.'

The stranger put his tee in the ground and followed suit while the world's worst golfer took over the commentary. 'That's a good shot, too!' he exclaimed. 'Over the bunker too, a little left of mine, but you'll probably get a shot in from there,' he encouraged. The pair marched off down the fairway, took out their irons, and both punched up onto the green. They followed their 'balls' up onto the green, took their putters out of their bags, and with two putts a piece, the 'balls' dropped in the hole. Great, they had each parred the hole. Finally they had played 17 holes and parred every hole, so the money was on the eighteenth, a par three. This hole went over a creek and was about 140 metres in length.

'Still your honour,' said the stranger. The world's worst golfer pulled his seven iron out of his bag, placed his tee in the ground, and went through the motions on the final hole. 'What a great shot,' screamed the stranger.

'Look, it's going straight for the flag. Oh, bad luck, the wind just got it at the end, and has dragged it across to the edge of the green. Pin high though, still a good shot!'

The stranger placed his tee in the ground, took out his seven iron, and swung.

'This is going to be a great shot too,' said the world's worst golfer. 'It's going towards the pin, look at this! Oh, what bad luck, the wind has got yours too, and it's dragged it across near mine. In fact, the two balls are side by side on the edge of the green.'

They marched up to the eighteenth green, and the world's worst golfer took out his putter, and lined it up from four or five different angles. Finally he stroked the imaginary ball.

'You've read the slope pretty well,' said the stranger. 'It's coming down the hill. Coming, coming, coming. It's in the hole. You've got a birdie!' he yelled, slapping the world's worst golfer on the back.

The stranger went over to his bag and pulled out his putter. He walked over to address his putt. 'Oh, what bad luck!' he suddenly exclaimed. 'You've gone and hit the wrong ball.'

Sometimes I think my golf is going so badly, I should give this a try myself.

Another story I like concerns David Hookes. His first Test for Australia was the 1977 Centenary Test Match in Melbourne. David had just hammered Tony Greig to all parts of the ground. He hit five fours in one over, and Tony wasn't very impressed by David's aggressive play. I'm sure no bowler would be, but anyway, Tony expressed his disapproval to this new young kid on a couple of occasions. Hooksie was never short of a word, and at this stage he replied, 'At least I'm an Australian, playing for my own country.' Tony didn't have much more to say to David. In fact, I don't think he ever bowled much more to him either.

A third story from some time ago has to do with the fact that I had a season or two with North Sydney back in the sixties. North Sydney was playing the newly formed Sutherland Cricket Club of which Norm O'Neill was a team member. He had just moved from the famous St George Club. At the time of this particular match, I also worked with Norm at Rothmans. In those days, we frequently parked in Miller Street, right outside the North Sydney Oval. Both Norm and I had left our Rothmans vehicles parked there to play in the match. A third person, Jack Adams, who worked for a subsidiary company of Rothmans, was umpiring the match. Norm was bowling when

I went out to bat. He decided to give me a wrong-un first ball. I played back to this ball, and missed, the ball going on to hit my back shin, plumb in front of middle stump. Norm wasn't at all happy when he appealed to Jack Adams and I was given not out. He decided to follow his first ball with a second wrong-un. I wasn't going to miss again, and over the fence it sailed, ending with a loud thump on someone's car bonnet.

Norm immediately turned to Jack and said, 'If that's my car, you're in trouble'. He later left the ground to find a large dent in it. He continued giving Jack a hard time for years after.

That famous St George Club I mentioned had more foresight than Cumberland, the other grade club I first played for. The story goes that in his younger days, Don Bradman wanted to travel from Bowral to Sydney to play grade cricket. Cumberland turned down his services rather than pay two shillings each week for his return train trip. Bradman ended up playing for St George.

The introduction of the third umpire along with neutral umpires will probably stop some of the really funny stories which have been told about umpiring decisions. I still laugh as I recall an incident which happened during my only tour of India, in 1969. The umpiring wasn't brilliant during that tour, but it was fair, and both sides got good and bad decisions. The way the umpires used to justify their decisions was hilarious. Ashley Mallett was one of our spin bowlers on this tour. He was well liked by the Indian public as well as the umpires. When we arrived at the Jaipur ground for a match against an Indian Zone side, we were met by the two umpires who were standing at the stairs of the bus as we alighted. They were introducing themselves to all the Australian players. I still have visions of one of these umpires telling our players how proud he was to be umpiring this, his first match. I'm sure he meant his first, first-class match, but this was lost in the translation.

Ashley Mallett followed behind me, and I was amazed to see

this umpire bowing several times to Ashley. Ashley returned the courtesy, and the umpire went on to tell him that he thought he was a great bowler, then quoted many of his figures and averages. We gathered that the umpire really admired Ashley because he was still telling him how wonderful he was as he carried Ashley's bags into the dressing room some five minutes later.

Not long after this, Bill Lawry had lost the toss, and we found ourselves out on the field. Because the wickets in India quickly take their toll on the new ball you can forget trying to polish it after the first one or two overs. I think this is where the idea of the reverse swing originated, although I'm still not convinced it didn't come from Richie Benaud and the Channel 9 crew. Bill Lawry had taken notice of the umpire's admiration for Ashley, and after the first two overs were bowled, Bill threw Ashley the ball and said, 'Hey, Rowdy [nicknamed because he was so quiet], you'd better have a bowl from your mate's end'. The two opening batsmen were still in, and after Ashley turned his first ball about a foot, the opener facing decided that the best form of defence should be attack. Ashley skipped in for his second delivery, and the little opener went charging down the wicket to try and get the ball on the half volley. As Ashley had seen him coming, he gave the ball a little more air and dropped it a little shorter.

The batsman was stranded three or four yards down the wicket when it spun back from way outside off-stump to wrap him on the pads. There are many bowlers who will appeal for everything, especially if the ball hits anywhere on a batsman's pad, but we always said Ashley would never die wondering whether the umpires might judge in his favour or not, as he always asks the question. He was the only one on the field who did appeal on this occasion, and his little mate raised his finger, saying, 'That's out'. Everyone else was too embarrassed to look anywhere near the umpire or Ashley, let alone congratulate him.

The opening batsman wasn't very impressed of course, but the umpire's finger was going up and down like a yo-yo, as they tend to do in India. Neither batsman, nor fielders could work out how the umpire could come to that decision, but eventually the opener had to leave as the next batsman had arrived at the crease and was ready to take guard. The number three batsman had obviously seen what had happened to the two previous deliveries and thought he would try the same tactics, but get down the wicket even further. Ashley tossed his next delivery even higher, shorter and wider. It, too, came spinning back and hit him on the pads. Ashley's confidence was sky high after the previous decision, and he nearly screamed his mate's head off with his appeal. Once more, he was the only one to do so. His mate the umpire, again raised his finger, and then walked across to where I was fielding at mid-off. 'This Mr Mallett's a very fine bowler,' he said, then followed it up by saying, 'That was his straight one.' There were no top spinners bowled by off-spinners in those days. Ashley somehow missed his hat-trick on that occasion.

This umpire can't have been thinking along the same lines as W.G. Grace is said to have been in a match where he was bowled first ball. W.G. politely bent down, picked up the bails, and replaced them on top of the stumps. Following this, he again took guard, saying, 'The people have all come here to watch me bat, not you bowl'.

Another story about India, which comes to mind, concerns John Gleeson. We called John, 'Cho' for 'Cricket Hours Only'. We didn't see a lot of him off the field. John was a very good finger spinner who copied the action of Jack Iverson, a master finger spinner in England in the fifties. John was a funny fellow from country NSW with down-to-earth country manners and wit. He was bowling in a match in Bangalore, India, when he got the outside edge and the ball was caught by our wicket-keeper, Ray Jordon. Ray was the second keeper on that tour. It was an obvious snick, which everyone appealed for. However, the umpire hesitated for what seemed like a couple of minutes. Cho eventually turned back to him and asked, 'Well, is he out, or isn't he?' The umpire pondered for another ten seconds before he finally put his finger up. The batsman in this case quite happily accepted his decision and marched off. The next batsman came out and played out the rest of the over. At the end of the over, as the umpire handed Cho his cap, he said, 'Mr Gleeson, I am very sorry it took so long for me to give that batsman out, but the wind was blowing in the opposite direction and it took some time for that snick to reach me'.

In that same match, Ray Jordon was given out, and he wasn't overly impressed with the umpire's decision. During the tea break Ray decided to question the umpire as to why he had been given out. Even Ray had to laugh at the umpire's reply, which was 'Oh, Mr Jordon, you were out twice'. 'What do you mean I was out twice?' asked Ray. 'Well,' said the umpire, 'if you didn't hit it, you were out LBW.'

Funny stories come from matches in Australia too. After a match in Perth where NSW had played Western Australia (and lost), Brian Taber and I were having a couple of beers and a game of pool in the pavilion bar. The match umpires joined us for a beer and challenged us to a game of pool. We decided to accept their challenge, even though one of the umpires had had a pretty ordinary game and had given a few doubtful decisions. This particular umpire aimed at the black ball, which was situated right over the corner pocket and missed. 'I'm playing this game just as badly as I'm umpiring,' he uttered. Brian wasn't all that happy about this comment, since he had been on the wrong end of one of those decisions. Anyway, we went on to win the game of pool so thought we had salvaged something from our trip to Perth.

I scored my last Test century against New Zealand at the MCG during the 1980–81 season. I actually think I can partly thank Jim Higgs and perhaps a match umpire for helping me score it. When I was in the 60s, a wicket fell, and Jim Higgs came into bat. We always said when Jim came in the heavy roller wasn't too far behind him. Jim wasn't exactly known for his batting. He was a spin bowler, and more recently, an Australian selector. Jim had actually gone through the entire 1975 tour of England without scoring one solitary run. I didn't hold very high hopes about scoring a century under these circumstances, but at least I knew Jim would try his hardest to stay there.

He played, and gloved a ball from Lance Cairns through to the wicket-keeper quite early in his innings. Everyone appealed, but the umpire gave him not out. In fairness to the umpire, it had been decided that short-pitched balls should not be bowled to players not recognized for their batting ability, otherwise it would be called a no-ball. The umpire duly did this. I did give some consideration to the decision, not that I doubted Jim's ability with the bat.

I think he qualified as a player not recognized for his batting ability, but I wondered whether Lance Cairns should be rated as a fast bowler. I really don't think he bowled much faster than Jim's leg spinners. Anyway Jim weathered that storm, and defended grimly for the next hour or so. I reached my century and was the last man out, clean bowled for 107. I turned, and headed for the dressing room.

Jim was still there, on 6 not out. When I was about halfway off the ground, I heard thumping footsteps behind me. I turned around as Jim touched me on the shoulder. I presumed he was about to congratulate me for getting a hundred, so I kept on walking. 'Hey!' Higgsy yelled. 'I did the right thing by you. The least you could have done was stick around till I got my century!' I replied, 'The Test match has only got three-and-a-half days to go, Jimmy'. Jim Higgs was a funny little fellow. He was nicknamed 'Glad'. This was because he used to turn up at cricket matches carrying garbage bags with all his cricket gear inside. Jim had no flash kit bag. I could understand why when I saw him pad up. He didn't own any pads, and had very little use for a bat, so why cart them around? Jim was the only fellow I've ever seen buckle his pads up from the top down. Buckles are not used on pads these days, but Jim probably wouldn't take any more care with the Velcro. I didn't see him pad up on the day he was six not out, but whatever he did gave him plenty of confidence, and I thank him for it.

I also like the story of a friend who was staying in Melbourne. He was waiting on a tram to go from St Kilda to the city and he decided to pre-purchase his ticket from the machine nearby. On boarding the tram, he handed his ticket to the conductor. The conductor looked at him and asked, 'What's this for?' My friend answered, 'It's my ticket from St Kilda to town'. The conductor then explained that it was no tram ticket, but a parking ticket. My friend had just fed someone's parking meter.

I shouldn't laugh at him, though, because a few years ago I hopped off a plane in Melbourne and walked out to the taxi queue. The taxis were arriving quickly, and I kept holding back and letting the people behind me go in front. One cabby, who had noticed me doing this a few times, pulled up and got out of his cab. 'Hey Doug, why are you letting all those people go ahead of you?' he asked. 'I'm in no hurry,' I replied. 'I decided to wait for a taxi I can have a smoke in.' 'You'll be waiting for a long time,' he said. 'They're all non-smoking down here.'

MEET THE SLOW FAST BOWLERS

*'. . . the ball hit him right on top of his head, cracking
down on his skull. It was a hole-in-one, and there's
no way I could repeat the performance if I tried
a thousand times.'*

Whenever you get a group of grown men together for an
extended period, travelling around the world and playing sport,
there are bound to be a few funny stories. Some you can print
and some you can't. Naturally some also lose humour in the
retelling and tend to fall into that 'you had to be there'
category. I hope these stories that follow, which are some of
my favourites, translate reasonably well onto the page.

Like front-row forwards in rugby league, fast bowlers carry
the tag of being a little thick upstairs. Rightly or wrongly, the
tag has stuck over the years and I can say that I have met a few

fast bowlers in my time who demonstrate that it isn't too far from the truth.

I remember one fast bowler, Mike Whitney, the big, barrel-chested quickie from Randwick, making a few of the boys laugh on tour in Hobart quite a few years ago. One of the big problems with a travelling cricket team is the laundry. Especially our playing whites and training gear. There's lots of it, for a start, and even though you fill in laundry slips stating what you have deposited for washing, you never seem to receive the same clothes back. Quite often you end up with someone else's socks, jocks, shirts and who knows what else. You also find, occasionally, that the person doing the laundry is a cricket fan and they decide to take a souvenir or two. A Shane Warne shirt, for example, might be quite a prize.

So, understandably, we have all learned it is wise to print our initial and surname inside our clothing. It is the easiest way of keeping track and identifying your clothes when the laundry comes back. Good thinking. Yet on one occasion this simple theory was put to the test. We were travelling around Australia and it was the start of the World Series Cup. It was a cold day in Hobart, and after a tough training session most of the team were pottering around in the dressing room getting all their gear together for the start of the series the next day.

There was Whit, sitting in the corner fiddling with his clothes and checking through to make sure he had everything in order. Most of you will pick up immediately that there are a couple of major differences between the Test match whites we wear and our one-day yellow uniforms. The major difference, apart from the colour, is the fact that our name and number is emblazoned across the back of our jumpers and shirts worn in the one-day games. You can't miss it.

Completely oblivious to this fact, however, there was Whit, carefully writing his name into the collars of all of his yellow shirts and jumpers. 'What are you doing, Whit?' I asked him.

'What do you think I'm doing, Junior?' he responded, as if I was the slightly slow one. 'I'm marking my shirts.'

'Well I'm sorry to disappoint you, Whit, but I think you're wasting your time. You'll find your name is already there.' With a wry smile he eventually got the point I was making and looked around the dressing room completely embarrassed.

Talking of fast bowlers having trouble with playing apparel, Glenn McGrath, our champion quickie, had some problems with his jumper on the 1997 Ashes Tour. It had been one of those frustrating days in a county match against Nottinghamshire. No rhythm, some lucky strokes from the batsman, a dropped catch or two, a cold, persistent breeze ripping through us, and a few bad decisions complete the picture. The opposition were 2 for 120, and nothing was going our way. To make matters even worse the English crowd were having great fun chanting out songs and indulging in a bit of cheeky banter. All you feel like doing in these situations is getting off the field and having a cup of tea and a hot bath. That was not to be, even after six hours out in the middle in those arctic conditions.

All of this can be hard to take, and Glenn McGrath certainly found the going tough, dealing with the crowd at fine-leg and going wicketless for two sessions. After tea on that day, amidst another spell, one particular over annoyed Glenn so much that he snatched his jumpers, both long-and short-sleeved, from the umpire without even looking at him. He didn't utter anything obscene or rude, he was just deeply frustrated with himself. Off he trotted, down to fine-leg, first putting his short-sleeved jumper on and then pulling his long-sleeved jumper over the top of it as he jogged towards the noisy crowd.

All of a sudden the crowd absolutely erupted. They were all laughing uncontrollably at Glenn. His first thought was that the laughter was aimed at his bowling and took even more offence. Noticing the noise, however, the rest of the players peered down at Glenn at fine-leg and we cast our eyes over a very funny sight. We all fell about too. Glenn had put his jumper on back-to-front and was completely unaware, as he remained absorbed in thought about his bowling. The team soon joined him, turning our jumpers around the wrong way too as an act of solidarity. Only then did Glenn get the picture. It certainly lightened up proceedings and gave the crowd a bit of entertainment on that bleak day.

This selection of fast bowler stories wouldn't be complete without one of my favourites about Merv Hughes. Funnily enough, Merv can actually bat a bit. One day he was playing a Shield game for Victoria and they were in a very tight spot, when Merv went in to bat. He took guard, and there were a lot of fieldsmen on the fence. Merv found himself facing a pretty good bowler. There was a lot of hope pinned on Merv's performance as he faced that first ball.

To everyone's disbelief, Merv unleashed a wild slog. The ball sailed long and high, but unfortunately landed in a fieldsman's hand on the long-on fence. He was out first ball, and in that one split second all the side's hopes were ruined. Merv came sauntering back in to face the wrath of his Captain, Simon O'Donnell, who said, 'Merv what the f*** were you doing out there mate? This is a tight game. How could you do that?' Merv looked at him, unconcerned, and replied, 'Gee, mate, haven't you ever had a good ball first up?'

Speaking of Simon O'Donnell, he had a joke he'd play on rookie interstate players on their first visit to Victoria. He'd tell them, when they first came to Melbourne, that the tram tracks were electrified and had to be avoided at all costs. Blokes would go around all week making sure they didn't step on the tram tracks. Apparently he caught Greg Ritchie out with this story. Ritchie hopped around and jumped over the tracks for days before anybody told him the truth.

Cricket, of course, all began in England, but the most fanatical supporters live in India. Indian cricketers are worshipped by their fans and are given god-like status in their country. Players like Tendulkar, Azharuddin, Gavaskar and Kapil Dev are mobbed whenever they set foot in public. Sponsors flood them with contracts, and the traffic literally stops when players are spotted in the cities. It's not just the Indian players either. Indian people respect and admire overseas players and put them up on almost as high a pedestal as their own players. We are treated like kings, with people carrying our bags and inviting us to restaurants and special functions. Everyone from taxi drivers to grandmothers know the faces of the Test cricketers.

Naturally, with the god-like status comes the desire of the locals to get as close as possible to the players. If they're in the right place at the right time, they'll follow you and ask for your autograph relentlessly. Once they've got the autograph they'll just hang around and watch you. A cricket souvenir like a training cap is very highly prized. The autograph is, however, the ultimate pursuit.

Autograph hunters the world over are a persistent lot. Some will do almost anything to get that autograph of their favourite player. They'll wait for hours and sometimes days. They'll travel long distances. They dodge traffic and security guards. Whatever it takes. Never more so than in India. The Indians are, without doubt, the most obsessed of all the cricket fans around the world.

Stephen, my brother, experienced the ultimate fanaticism of this kind during the last World Cup in India. We were staying at a really exceptional hotel in Calcutta and had been made extremely welcome. There was plenty of security to keep non-guests out of the hotel, but the autograph hunters were out in force. We always do as much as we can to accommodate as many as possible. Stephen is no different in this regard and, as with all of us, he'll stand signing for long periods of time. Quite often, though, you are being hurried along to practice or a function and the line has to be drawn somewhere. It just isn't humanly possible to get to everyone.

One of the locals had been chasing Stephen for days, following him everywhere and never letting up. He was really crowding Stephen, who eventually told him, in no uncertain and unprintable terms, to leave him alone.

The fan had become testy after this rebuke, but Stephen was evidently equally testy with him. Eventually the fan decided to retaliate shrewdly and verbally, and when he next saw Stephen he said, 'Excuse me, Mr Wog [Waugh], can I be having your autograph or should I be f*****g off?' For showing such a sense of humour, the India fan eventually got his autograph and went away happy.

My pursuit of a hole-in-one at golf is equal to these obsessive lengths of the autograph hunters. I have never managed to get a hole-in-one, but it is something I would dearly love to do. After years of trying, I've only come close. I have, however, completed the cricket equivalent of a hole-in-one during a tour to Sri Lanka.

Australia was touring there for the Singer Cup, a one-day tournament played between Sri Lanka, Pakistan and Australia. It was a practice day and we had a centre wicket practice. This means the groundsman had set the nets up on the square out in the middle rather than behind the grandstands, which is traditional in Australia.

There were a few people watching behind the nets—a couple of journalists and photographers, and some keen local players trying to pick up some tips from our guys. In the grandstands, which were quite a long distance away from where we are practising at that very large ground (almost the equivalent of the MCG), there were a few cleaners getting the stadium ready for the next day by picking up rubbish, wiping down seats and occasionally watching us practice. Nevertheless, the stand was, for all intents and purposes, empty.

I was having a bat and trying to simulate match conditions by going after the spinners and trying to hit a few sixes. Some

I miscued and some I didn't. Then, on one of my shots I hit it right out of the middle with my Slazenger V100 and amazingly it went a very long way. It travelled over the fence and headed to about halfway up the first tier of the grandstand. As I watched the ball travel, I noticed in the distance a cleaner standing right in the line of the flight of the ball. He really was a long way off and, as I looked at him, I thought he was watching the ball coming towards him and would either catch it or move out of the way. He had time to take up one of these options.

As it happened, though, he didn't move at all, and the ball hit him right on top of his head, cracking down on his skull. It was a hole-in-one, and there's no way I could repeat the performance if I tried a thousand times. The unfortunate man ran like a startled rabbit for 20 metres before crashing to the ground in immense pain. The ball ricocheted some 10 metres in the air after it struck his head. I was utterly horrified and extremely worried for him.

I rushed over to check on his state of health. He still lay on the ground holding his head but looked up at me when I offered him a brand new pair of autographed gloves. I apologised at length for the incident when it appeared that, although he was hurt, he was going to survive. By now you are probably wondering how this unfortunate man's tale fits into a chapter containing our funniest stories, but stay with me.

My unwitting victim eventually looked up at me calmly and said, 'Mr Wog, it is a pleasure to be hit by you and thank you for the gloves. Perhaps a helmet would be more useful next time?'

Well, that's it. I hope you're not groaning at this point. There are plenty more where they came from, but I'll spare you the pain. I just hope Douggie's are better.

CHAPTER TWELVE

SPORTSMANSHIP

SLEDGING IS BORN

*'The wives and children soon retreated to the house to
seek refuge while the two contestants gave their all.'*

The word 'sledging' wasn't around when I first started playing
first-class cricket, although gamesmanship was often mentioned. I can, however, remember that the new term originated
in the backyard of Huck Finn's home in Adelaide. I know that
sounds fictional, but I swear it is true.

Huck Finn was the president of the Glenelg Cricket Club in
the late 1960s and early '70s. Ian and Greg Chappell and later
Trevor Chappell all played for Glenelg. When the NSW team
were playing South Australia, we were often invited to Huck
Finn's home for a fundraising evening for the Glenelg Cricket
Club. I went along to two or three of these nights on various
trips to Adelaide with the NSW side.

On one of the nights, Ian Chappell told us that the club's

opening batsman was the best swearer he had ever come across. He assured us that this man gave all the bowlers a run for their money and he could add to the night's entertainment. John Benaud was the NSW captain at the time and he pricked up his ears when he heard Ian talking about the opening bat. He assured Ian that a member of the NSW team was also a very good swearer, and he was 'as subtle as a sledgehammer'.

Between them, they decided that Geoff Davies (the NSW nomination) and the Glenelg opening bat should stand toe-to-toe in the middle of Huck's backyard to see who was the best. They were to be given equal time, about two minutes.

The biggest problem was that it was a mixed function, and many Glenelg players not only had their wives with them, but also their children, plus mothers and anyone else they could con into going, to help raise money for the club. Huck Finn's back-yard was not an appropriate place for many of the people, once the contest started. The wives and children soon retreated to the house to seek refuge while the two contestants gave their all. In the end, Geoff Davies was unanimously crowned the 'King Sledge'.

Word travelled overnight to the Adelaide Cricket Ground, and, I'm sure, to the Glenelg Cricket Ground as well. It seemed to only take a couple of weeks before it travelled to every cricket ground in the world. It didn't stop at cricket grounds either. It has popped up on golf courses, football grounds, tennis courts and I actually can't think of a sport where it isn't known and used. It still goes on. Unfortunately, the word 'gamesmanship' disappeared overnight when 'sledging' took over.

People often ask me whether the sledging is any better or worse these days. I really don't think things have changed a great deal in that department. As I explained, it's only the terminology that has changed. Perhaps the players of today have to be a little more discreet because there are microphones

I was born 1.8 kilograms heavier than my twin brother, Stephen, but it looks like he's got my measure here. I'm playing under him again now he's captain. *Courtesy: News Limited*

The day before my Test debut in the 1991 Australia Day Test in Adelaide. Definitely one of the high points of my career.
Courtesy: News Limited

Discussing tactics with Mark Taylor during the second Test, India v Australia in Calcutta, 1998. Mark was a fantastic captain and a calming influence on the players.
Courtesy: Craig Prentis and Allsport Australia

With Ricky Ponting in Northern Ireland in 1997. *Courtesy: Clive Mason and Allsport Australia*

Off and racing in Bermuda in 1995. *Courtesy: Mark Waugh*

At the races in Barbados with Ricky Ponting in 1995.
Courtesy: Mark Waugh

Receiving a silver medal at the Commonwealth Games in Kuala Lumpur in 1998. The gold medal winners, South Africa, are to the right.
Courtesy: Mark Waugh

With one of my winning horses, Oblico, at the Harold Park Paceway. The driver is Glenn Frost. *Courtesy: Lett Photography*

At the stables
discussing tactics
with another one
of my horses.
*Courtesy: Mark
Waugh*

Viv Richards is my
all-time favourite
player and always
has been. *Courtesy:
Adrian Murrell and
Allsport Australia*

Shane Warne and I going into the press conference held during the 'Bookie Scandal'. This was the lowest point of my career.
Courtesy: Graham Chadwick and Allsport Australia

Opposite page: Ian Healy after hitting *that* six in Port Elizabeth in March 1997 to win the second Test and the series. We really celebrated that one. *Courtesy: Mark Waugh*

JNR
I WISH 'IT WERE
YOU, MATE!

Nowadays the media is always there, even at practice, as you can see here in Adelaide in December 1998.
Courtesy: Laurence Griffiths and Allsport Australia

Here I am being bounced by Allan Donald. I'd definitely have him in my dream team. *Courtesy: Ben Radford and Allsport Australia*

Making a century in the fifth Test against England at the SCG in
January 1999. I was playing instinctively at that point because I had so
much else going on in my life.
Courtesy: Clive Mason and Allsport Australia

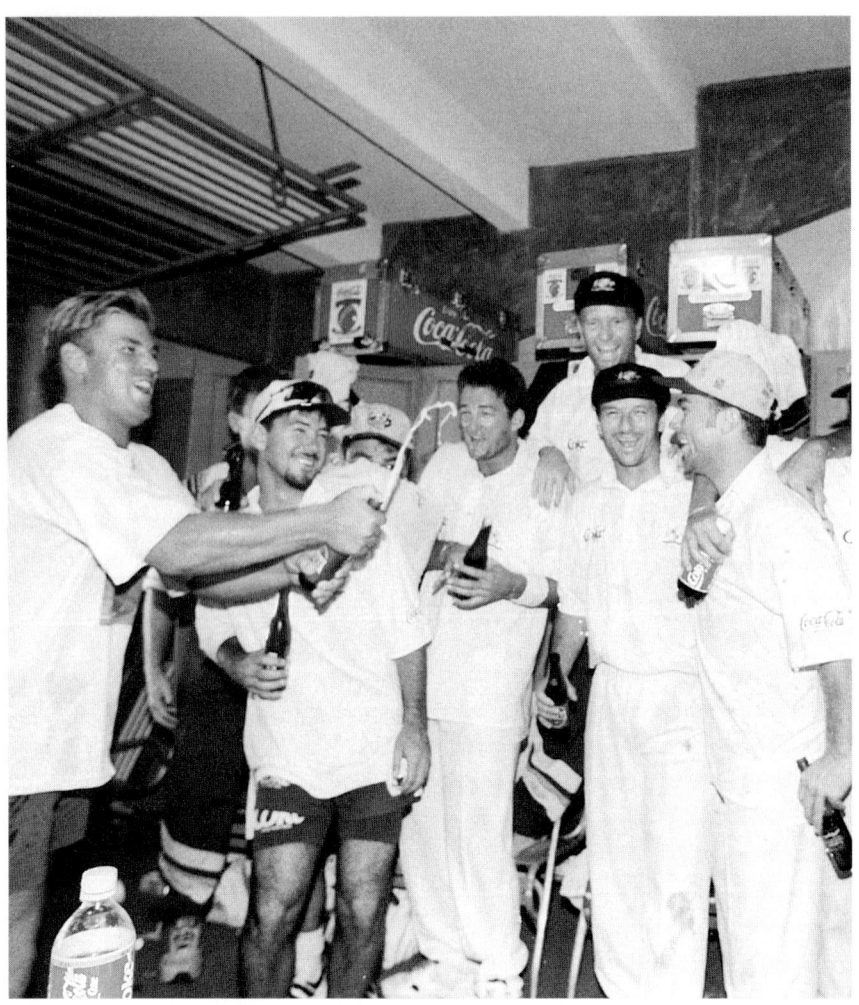
The team knows how to celebrate. Here we are in Barbados in 1995 after a Test victory. *Courtesy: Mark Waugh*

Shaking hands with Hansie Cronje at the end of the third Test in Adelaide in 1998. We have a very good relationship with the South African team. *Courtesy: Ben Radford and Allsport Australia*

The 'girls' on tour. Wives and partners are a welcome presence on tour and they also know how to celebrate as they demonstrate here during the 1999 World Cup in England. My fianceé, Sue, is second from the right (seated). *Courtesy: Mark Waugh*

Celebrations after the 1999 World Cup in Melbourne at the Crown Casino. John Williamson and Molly Meldrum bring some harmony to the team's less than dulcet tones. *Courtesy: Mark Waugh*

Darren Lehmann and me proudly showing off the World Cup after our win in June 1999. *Courtesy: Mark Waugh*

On the way to my highest score in Test cricket, 153 not out against India, in the third Test in Bangalore in 1998.
Courtesy of Shaun Botterill and Allsport Australia

in the stumps, and people are pretty good at lip reading off their television sets, but they still get the message across.

Contests will always continue to bring out heated clashes with people, whether it's in cricket or any other sport. Providing it stays at one-on-one, it is not too bad, but problems arise when other team members join in. The situation gets right out of hand if that happens. Over the years there have been some ugly incidents where other team members have joined in disputes, and this is not good for any sport. These days, the penalties handed out for carrying such incidents too far have helped to blunt player enthusiasm for trouble. I think good umpires are the secret as they can stop minor scuffles in their infancy.

Dickie Bird was the best umpire I came across for putting an end to disputes. He had tremendous respect from all the players, and once Dickie intervened, that was the end of the conversation. It is a great pity that we don't have more Dickie Birds around.

I don't mind a little sledging on the cricket fields as long as it stays on the ground. When players don't mix with the opposition teams like they used to after stumps each day, there is little chance to talk out the on-field problems, away from the heat of the moment. I always felt that many potential incidents could be defused this way. A laugh over a few beers at the end of each day often fixed everything in my playing days. There were occasions when this didn't happen and the feuds continued.

Ian Chappell had a reputation for being a good sledger. I felt that he wasn't being unfair. He would talk to a player or an umpire so that the opposition bowler could hear him and become angry before his delivery. I personally believed that the bowlers already bowled fast enough without upsetting them, but Ian reckoned that they lost their accuracy when they were riled up. I think Ian's tactics grew from his baseball days.

In my early years of state and Australian cricket, I also played baseball, as did most cricketers. It was felt that baseball helped to keep your 'eye in'. I'm not sure that it worked for me because I always felt that the baseball bat wasn't wide enough for me. Sledging was then, and I guess still is, a big part of baseball. I always felt opposition players would try anything to put the pitcher off his line. Ian was a top catcher in baseball, so he wasn't trying to upset his pitchers.

Sledging can get out of hand, as it did a couple of times when NSW were playing South Australia. Yes, Ian was the captain of South Australia and I was the captain of NSW, however, we still remain the best of mates. When Ian reached his half-century during one such Shield match (on his way to 158), his younger brother, Trevor, who was playing for NSW said, 'That's the best 50 I've ever heard'. Ian believed that, whether on the cricket or the baseball field, everyone was fair game, but he was the first one to have a beer with the opposition at the end of the day's play.

I think it shows great sportsmanship when a fielder recalls a batsman who has been given out to a catch that was not completed. Captains have done this too. The umpires are only human and they do make mistakes, not seeing balls bouncing close to the ground. Any help they can be given is of benefit to the game. The third umpire and television replays have stopped a lot of arguments about decisions. Arguments often don't only occur between players, but spectators as well. When people outside the playing field become involved, the incidents can become very nasty.

Crowds in India and Pakistan were famous for this, but it's good to see that they now accept the decisions in better style. I saw some bad incidents during our tour of India in 1969. I never want to experience crowd behaviour like that again. There was hardly any television coverage in those days and, consequently, very few replays, so people made instant decisions. I can tell you that with people rioting, burning chairs, grandstands, and the like, I wasn't enjoying playing my sport.

It's pretty hard on occasions to accept the umpire's decision, particularly when your career hangs on the outcome of your team's result. I always used to tell myself that there would always be another day dawning tomorrow, before saying anything to anyone else, and I always calmed down fairly quickly. You never know, the umpire's future could be under a bigger cloud than yours.

To be able to recognize someone else's success before your own is something I advise all cricketers of all ages to do. It is a lot easier to say one good word than to criticize. Always let your mates know that you appreciate their efforts. I would also advise all parents to let their children enjoy playing sport and refrain from being critical of their own, or other people's children as well. When people make mistakes they want encouragement to try again, not criticism that reminds them of their mistakes.

I often see and hear far too much from parents who think they are helping their children. More often, what these people are doing is driving their children away from sport. It is important that children are involved in sport, so we need to do all we can to encourage them.

PASSION PLAY

*'They said "You can't play the short ball. You're soft," and
made other fairly gentle remarks along similar lines.'*

I believe that in international cricket, the players from around
the world mostly respect each other. After all, this is our livelihood and we all take it very seriously. There isn't a lot of time
or opportunity for abusing each other. We're there to play. In
any case, the match referee and the camera would be right onto
us even if we wanted to do or say anything. I am, of course,
talking about sledging. Match referees appointed to each game
also ensure that the code of conduct and sportsmanship is
adhered to.

That's not to pretend that there isn't a little bit of it around.
We are playing for our countries and, inevitably, there are
intense feelings in the game. That is the way it should be. The
passion is important.

In any sport, there are words spoken in anger between players, whether it's rugby league, cricket or basketball. Nevertheless, for as long as I've been playing at the top level, there's been very little talk out there. There haven't been any incidents of a sledging nature that have ever really upset me or that I've witnessed upsetting someone else to any great extent.

To be honest, on the few occasions when someone has sledged me, I've really enjoyed it. It has fired me up and made me more determined to succeed. Against South Africa in 1998, there was a little bit of sledging on the last day when I went out to bat. Pat Symcox and Hansie Cronje said a few things, and I absolutely loved it. I really got going and, from memory, I did well that day. They said 'You can't play the short ball. You're soft,' and made other fairly gentle remarks along similar lines.

I know they were trying to put me off my game and break my concentration. All it did, though, was spur me on to perform better.

Players will try and put you off your game as you take centre or face up to bat. Some batsmen are completely put off by it. It can distract a player if you talk about their weaknesses, and players do sometimes make sly comments about the shots another player can't play. I don't actually call this sledging. To me it is gamesmanship and is as old as the game itself. We definitely need to make the distinction between outright abusive sledging, which is extremely rare and obviously unacceptable, and the more likely, and much more strategic, gamesmanship.

As long as it's not personal or you're not being racist, I don't have a problem with a bit of gamesmanship. There wouldn't be a player who hasn't made some comment at some time. I think the controversy which flares up every now and again about sledging in cricket is due to the fact that this is the 'gentlemen's game'.

It does seem to be frowned upon in cricket more than in other sports, although football codes have been coming in for some of the scrutiny more recently. I still maintain, however, that it has always been part of the game and always will be. Just look at Bodyline! There would certainly have been words spoken during the Bodyline series, and I wouldn't mind betting that my co-author, Douggie, has witnessed a bit of sledging in his day.

The Dennis Lillee–Javed Miandad incident in Perth where bats and legs were flying everywhere is one that comes to mind. When Australia played the West Indies and beat them 5–1 in the days of Thommo and Lillee, I think the Aussies really took it to the West Indies both verbally and physically and I don't think it's ever been forgotten. We really copped a bit back from them for quite a few years.

I can remember coming in to bat and they'd be saying 'Come on, let's knock his head off'. Ambrose, in particular, used to get me out all the time, and I'd come in to bat with Viv Richards calling out to Ambrose, 'Come on Ambie, he's your meat, man. He's all yours.' That sort of thing can be really intimidating. It's done completely without swearing or being personal or abusive. It's all in the words that are chosen and the way they're delivered. That sort of thing doesn't look bad on the TV screen at all. They'd be completely calm. Staring at us is another weapon they used. Really, they don't have to say much at all when the ball is whizzing past your head at 100 miles an hour. That's bad enough. You're already thinking the worst.

Our current team is very quiet. If you were to ask players from other countries, they'd tell you we say very little. Don't ask the media though because they seem to have the impression that we sledge all the time. Maybe there are cases for saying that Glenn McGrath and Shane Warne occasionally go close to stepping over the mark, but in my opinion, they are just great competitors.

Several articles over the last few years have been, I believe, a beat up. If you were judging from the stories that appear, Ian

Healy and Stephen are very big sledgers. That just isn't the case. They may make the occasional fairly strategic remark but, over-all, they just get on with the game. I know we've been given the wrong tag as the 'world's biggest sledgers'.

There are bound to be a few incidents. We're not playing local netball after all. It's not trial cricket. It's the real thing at the top level, and people are under pressure. Merv Hughes was a great example of a player at that level who used gamesman-ship in a more open way than most of us. I enjoyed it when he'd run up to opposition players and just stare at them. He was also one of the few players I've ever played with who would say things to a batsman. Most of the time it was light-hearted. Some very mild swearing but never, ever in real anger or being truly abusive. It's a line he didn't cross, but he was great at intimidating players.

Warnie's very good at gamesmanship too. Even though he's a spin bowler he can intimidate guys in lots of other subtle ways. When we played Pakistan a few years ago, it was the last ball of the day and he was bowling to Basit Ali. Warnie called Heals over and they just talked for a couple of minutes in a sort of secretive way. They didn't actually talk about anything at all, but the batsman clearly thought they were planning. Ali certainly felt something big was going to happen and they also kept the batsman waiting nervously on the last ball of the day.

On the next ball, Warnie bowled him around the legs, and all the journalists were writing what a great plan it had been to bowl him around his legs, but in fact our two players hadn't discussed any plan at all. It was just pure gamesmanship. Making the batsman wait and making him nervous.

Obviously this tactic can't work often and it would slow the game down terribly if it was on all the time. That's just the point. It is a tactical part of the game which I think is very acceptable, but it is a small part and always will be.

I actually think sportsmanship is alive and well in the game of cricket, despite some occasional ugly incidents. If we make a century, all the players on both sides clap and show that they respect the way you've played.

I admit, however, that there are times when the spirit of sportsmanship is perhaps not as strong in certain teams. There are teams that scratch the ball to make it swing, and there are players who'll call for a runner when they're not hurt and don't need a runner. That sort of thing is obviously bad for the game and should be stamped out.

Then there are the teams who move fieldsmen when the bowler is running in to bowl, and there are teams that substitute good fieldsmen for bad fieldsmen. They'll bring on their best players in the one-dayers, saying they've got injured players. There are players who'll dig up the wicket by running down it in their spikes. These are the problems that should be stamped out by the ICC. To me they are more prevalent and much worse than the present level of verbal sledging which is, as I have explained, not very common at all.

Scratching the ball up is out-and-out premeditated cheating. I won't name the teams that employ these practices but they are there and they get away with it often.

I think the ICC is too preoccupied with stopping players from swearing, instead of dealing with the major problems I've described. Clearly they are more worried about the behaviour that is obvious to the public and can be picked up by the cameras, than they are about the more serious but hidden problems.

Take Daryll Cullinan when he was given out for handling the ball in a one-dayer between South Africa and the West Indies. He hit the ball, and it wasn't going to hit the stumps, so he picked it up and threw it back to the bowler. The West Indies appealed and he was given out. To me that sort of thing leaves a bad taste in your mouth. I don't think it needs to go like that if we all respect each other. There was no need for them to appeal in that situation. Commonsense must prevail in these types of incidents.

These days there are also lots of players trying to intimidate the umpire by appealing all the time when they know the batsman isn't out. In this respect, the game sometimes gets a little out of hand. Of course you want to win, but appealing loudly when you know it's not out is cheating. This should be stamped out and the ICC is trying to do just that. It must still be kept in perspective—these incidents being few and far between in the many, many hours of Test cricket being played around the world.

Overall, though, there is a good feeling out there on the field. There's little serious sledging, but it is a very tough and pressured atmosphere. You're playing for money and glory. You're playing for your place in the team. Obviously a winning team is more likely to stay intact, so winning is of the utmost importance, and you can feel the intensity of the battle out there in the middle.

There isn't too much joking or mucking around. We don't often break concentration. I think this has changed over the years and I'll be interested to learn how Doug feels about this subject. I have a feeling there was more banter and obvious enjoyment in the playing of the game back then. Now it's straight-down-the-line serious stuff. I'm not out there thinking up lines to use on my opponents, and neither is anyone else.

Most of the teams get along pretty well with each other. After games we tend to have a drink with the other side. Australia, New Zealand, Zimbabwe, England and South Africa seem to mix better with each other than with India, Pakistan, West Indies and Sri Lanka. It's just a cultural and language difference. We've grown up so differently from each other. The gaps are smaller between the first group of teams I mentioned.

You still say hello to all teams of course and it is friendly, but it can also become awkward if we're having long conversations with the latter group because we usually have very little in common other than cricket.

South Africa is the team I'd say Australia gets on with best. They have a similar disposition to us. We play it tough, but once off the field we forget about it, and have a drink and a yarn. They're our toughest opponents on the field and our best off-field friends among all the teams. There's a strong mutual respect there.

There isn't as much interaction between teams as there used to be when I first started playing. You're playing each other so much and seeing each other so often that you don't necessarily feel like a get-together after a game. Frankly, you mostly feel like going home after a ten-hour day of cricket.

At the start of a series, you usually find you're better friends with the opposition than you are at the end of a series. Mostly it all starts off very well, with the captains getting us all together and we all make an effort. After the first Test we'll interact socially, but by the third Test, that early friendliness has worn off a bit on both sides. If a bloke's trying to knock your head of all day, you don't necessarily want to make small talk with him over drinks. That's natural. By the end of a series you mostly want to see the back of each other.

CHAPTER THIRTEEN

GOING PROFESSIONAL

NO REGRETS

'The players' code of behaviour has changed today. I don't think it was ever out of control, but I'm sure I would have to change my habits a great deal if I was still playing today.'

I was led to believe that I was the first since Sir Donald Bradman to get a thousand pounds for my signature on a cricket bat. I went on to wonder what went wrong in the end because the thousand pounds became $2,000 in 1966 when the currency changed, however by 1980–81, when I retired, I was only earning $500 per season for the same signature—even though, by then, match payments were improving dramatically.

It seemed that while improvements were happening in some ways, other player benefits were actually going backwards. Many more players were starting to gain a share of the money, which bat manufacturers offered as player sponsorship. However, there were some players like Gary Gilmour, a very talented left-hand all-rounder, who had scored a Test century yet didn't receive a cent from a bat manufacturer. He retired a couple of seasons before I did, but still, to play at that level for a number of years with such success, I thought should have warranted a greater financial reward.

I am told that the players of today do very well from such sponsorships and can receive payments for many things that can vary from wearing particular sunglasses, to more traditional necessities, such as boots. The match payments have gone ahead in leaps and bounds, as I feel they should have.

I consider myself lucky to have played at the time of World Series Cricket, and then I played in an additional six Test matches after it finished. Prior to the commencement of World Series Cricket, Austin Robertson and John Cornell had asked me what I had earned out of cricket in the previous 12 months. That year had been particularly busy, as it included a tour of England and a tour of New Zealand, as well as the Australian summer, so it involved playing cricket for nearly a full year. When I added up all of the match payments and sponsorships for that year, it totalled a grand $5,000. I was in my thirties at this stage, so you can see that when I was offered five times that much to join World Series, my decision was an easy one to make.

Joining involved signing a contract, which required me to play for three seasons. As it turned out, World Series only lasted for two seasons. I had worked for Rothmans for about 12 years at this stage. They had been very good employers in that they gave me time off for practice as well as the time I needed to play for NSW and Australia, and they had given me leave while I served my time in the National Service. If it hadn't been for companies like Rothmans, cricketers would not have been able to play for their state or country because match payments were far from sufficient to live on.

World Series Cricket meant that players became professionals and could not give their time to a job as well, and besides that, many companies remained loyal to the Cricket Board, so did not wish to continue to employ players who had signed up. World Series Cricket involved going into a camp situation, unless we were playing in our hometown, and we were transported by either bus or plane.

This was different to just being away for specific matches, but wives and children were made very welcome, so the longer stretches away from home did not worry me at all. By today's standards, I guess my sign-on fee was very small, even for current Sheffield Shield players, but I think if it hadn't happened, things would not have changed too much as far as remuneration for players anyway.

My retirement fund more than doubled as a result of the increase in payments made for the six Test matches I played after World Series finished. It suddenly totalled more than I had accumulated for the 69 Test matches I had played previously. My package, just the same, was hardly a fortune, adding up to around $10,000. Contracts with the Australian Cricket Board began about this time too. I was never offered one, and I didn't really agree with the concept because I felt—and still do—that players should not be paid unless they play. It's hard to know what the correct balance is, but higher match payments and a superannuation fund for matches played might be more like the arrangement I would aim for, rather than seasonal contracts. As it is now, though, very few players have jobs as well, so I guess the contracts help ensure that they keep themselves fit and ready to play. However, I also feel that the large payments of today put more pressure on the players to perform consistently, as there is the necessity to have the contract renewed when they don't really have another job to go to after cricket.

When I played, I didn't feel that I did so for the monetary rewards it would give me. I honestly think I would have taken the chance to play for Australia for no money at all, but as the years went on, and the number of matches increased, it became more and more difficult to maintain a home and a job. They are playing an incredible number of matches these days, by comparison with the number I was playing in any one year. I guess the cricket played must have also changed. I actually think this has been the case with all sports once money has become an issue.

I do believe we played for the team more, rather than for ourselves as individuals. It wasn't really the end of our lives and our whole income if we were not selected. I think the enjoyment of sport, just in playing a game, goes, once money is involved. I'm not saying today's players don't enjoy their cricket, but it is definitely different, not only in the number of Test and one-day series. I think, overall, I'm happy to have played cricket in the era that I did. Today I would have to change my outlook on the game. Where I can say I played for the team on all occasions— varying from aggressive to defensive play, depending on the situation of the team—players of today really need to look after their own interests first and foremost.

The extra dollars are also available off the field, and this brings added pressures and commitments, which I didn't really have to contend with. Today the game requires a greater level of fitness from all players than when I played. However, there were players who were exceptions to this in my time. I find it difficult to believe that anyone could be fitter than Dennis Lillee was.

The fitness level of today shows clearly in the fielding, rather than either the batting or the bowling. We practised fielding when I played for NSW and Australia, but not to the extent that they do now. Training began to change towards the end of my playing career and Norm O'Neill asked me one day, after we started having to run around ovals and do a number of other fitness routines, 'Does all that running improve your cover drives?' To answer his question honestly, I guess it doesn't, but if you're back in the dressing room, having got out through lack of fitness, and consequently not batting at all, then you can't hope to play any shots.

Prior to World Series Cricket, most of our practice sessions were done in the nets, along with some fielding and catching practice. Fast bowlers also did some roadwork. Gymnasiums were not even considered by most players. We did practise hard, although not for as long as the players of today. I had a reputation for not being great at practice, but this is not entirely true as I was often the first to arrive and the last to leave on the days which were set aside as practice days. However, I also felt that if you were still worried about your form on the morning of a match, then you had really big problems.

Another reason why I often chose not to go to the nets on the morning of a match was that I believed that I was supposed to be a batsman, not a ground bowler, which is what I had to be on most mornings that I went. I also felt that with six hours' play ahead, often very hot hours at that, I didn't need another two hours' bowling in the nets. This didn't make any sense to me at all, particularly if I only got to face a half dozen balls, if I was lucky. I frequently noticed that someone threw these few balls from only halfway down the wicket, so I quickly became tired of this form of practice.

The players' code of behaviour has changed today. I don't think it was ever out of control, but I'm sure I would have to change my habits a great deal if I was still playing today. It seems that some members of the press wait for players to do something which is considered out of the norm, and then the publicity is unbelievable. Players understandably believe that it is not worth the risk of being seen playing up in public 'out of hours', as this would give some members of the press a good enough reason to bag the player's performance on the field for only small errors.

Players of today don't mix nearly as well with the opposing teams as we did when I was playing. This could have something to do with the fact that they play them far more often, but I always felt that I learned a lot more in the opposition dressing rooms if I spent an hour or two in there after each day's play. Sometimes I thought that it was more than I had learned during the previous six hours on the field.

I feel it goes back to where I mentioned that players are the best coaches once they reach this level of cricket. Players from opposing teams would happily share advice that could be helpful, but I couldn't see this happening today.

Sponsorships are playing a more important role in cricket now. Like most sports, cricket seems to be scheduled to fit into television commitments. This professional aspect has become more apparent since the beginning of World Series Cricket. Kerry Packer quickly told us that we were being paid as professionals and we should act accordingly. At one of our first team meetings after the formation of World Series Cricket, we were lectured on the topic of professionalism by John Newcombe and Ron Barassi. Newk had come through the hard school, but by this time, he was earning a lot more than all of us put together. We were hardly in the same league as him, but he did give us a number of sound points.

Ron gave us examples of various teams that he had coached and pointed out the reasons why some of them had not always performed as expected. I actually found it amusing and began to chuckle when he told us that some of his players had eaten meat pies and drank malted milkshakes early in the week. He went on to say that others weren't in bed by 8.30pm the night before a game. I thought he had to be joking but he was deadly serious, and I began to worry that this would never work for me. The malted milkshakes wouldn't be a problem, but a few other points sounded very uncharacteristic for me.

A few years later, I met Ron when we were making a Four 'n' Twenty pie ad together, and I didn't let him forget the solemn lecture he had given at the start of the 1977–78 season. I rubbed in the fact that he also owned a pub, not a milkbar. I can understand that nutrition is important for many athletes, but for cricket, I think a basic diet is ample to allow one to take wickets and score runs.

BRAVE NEW WORLD

'In the end, despite what some people say about the distraction of working for sponsors and chasing the dollars, it is all about performance on the field.'

The new professionalism and the amount of money we can earn now has obviously been a striking change since the days when Doug played Test cricket. In Doug's day, I suspect a lot of the players had other jobs as well, which would be impossible for us these days. Nor do we have to have another job because we can do very well out of cricket. At any rate, companies these days cannot afford to have employees taking off for cricket training at 3.00pm or going away for five consecutive days for a Shield or Test match.

Having said that, we also play much more cricket and play in a much more pressured environment. You can have quite a few years at the top of the game, as long as you don't get seriously injured, although history tells you that only a few blokes will have more than a hundred Tests. I don't think there will be many blokes in the next few years who will even play that many because of the increase in the number of games we're playing. Specifically, I'm talking about lots more one-day cricket. Players could become injured or burnt out from overplaying, and their careers may well be shorter at the top because of it.

There simply isn't any time off anymore. We play because we love the game, but at this level with that pressure, we play for our livelihood too. It is a relatively short career compared with other people's working lives in their chosen fields, so you are very conscious of making the most of it while it's happening, and that means finding sponsors and projecting a good image while you can! I know Doug believes that having to earn a living from cricket and your sponsors has created a more self-ish cricketer these days. I know he has suggested that we might worry about our selves first and the team second. I can't agree with him because I don't think a team would survive or do well with this attitude.

At present, the Australian team is having a golden run, especially in the Test arena. The reason for this, in my opinion, is the combination of a group of talented players who enjoy each other's success and play for each other. There may be the odd individual who puts himself first occasionally, but ninety-nine percent of the time, the team comes first.

In the end, despite what some people say about the distraction of working for sponsors and chasing the dollars, it is all about performance on the field. If you don't perform you don't attract the sponsors and you don't make the money. There's no getting around the fact that cricket absolutely comes first. No question about it. Even if making money was your only objective, the cricket has to come first or you'll end up earning nothing.

The bottom line is to worry about your cricket first and fore-most. That's what I do, and I'm pretty sure I also speak for the other players in the Australian side. If you're playing good cricket, the money looks after itself—the ACB contract will be there and the sponsors will come.

We all know Warnie is on a completely different level to the rest of us, but we all have sunglasses and footwear contracts, and the batsmen have their bat sponsorships. You basically get what you've worked for. The longer you've been around, the higher your profile and the more likely you are to attract sponsors. Obviously this doesn't always hold true and it certainly doesn't when you've retired.

Nevertheless, all of this comes at a price. The days of relaxing after practice with a beer are gone. Now it's all skin-fold tests, nutrition and extra training, whether it's in the gym or in the pool. When I first started, there was so much more time off and we'd go and have a relaxing game of golf. I didn't play golf once in the summer of 1998–99 and that's a major change. I'm not complaining at all, because I know I'm in a very privileged position and I have to work to maintain it, but I want to show how the extra rewards are certainly well earned.

We have a full-time fitness advisor in David Misson, a nutritionist who looks after our waistlines, and a sports psychologist, all recent additions to the team during the last couple of years. Every avenue is explored in the pursuit of fitness.

The commitments to sponsors, once you have them, are also very demanding. In addition to individual sponsorships, we have obligations to ACB sponsors too. There are several Carlton & United Breweries and Ansett functions to attend and we always have bat-signing sessions. There are very few spare days. To have two days off in a row in a year is rare. It must be extremely hard for players with children and even harder for the wives. Good sponsors are hard to find, so the players are happy to fulfil commitments and give sponsors value for money.

On the subject of cricket skills, when I started we'd have a hit in the nets at practice and then the rest of the day off. The new professionalism has changed that approach, and now we have a compulsory swim, and lots of meetings to talk about the opposition players and your own game. Sometimes I think we go overboard. In the 1998–99 season we have had a meeting before every single one-day game, though we've played exactly the same team five times. Even last year, we would only have such a meeting before the first game. So every season it's becoming more intense and it's hard to see where it will lead. No stone is left unturned.

Nothing is left to chance anymore. A day's training could involve nets and fielding in the morning until lunch. Then we have a gym and swim session in the early evening. When I'm actually doing all this training, I think to myself, 'Can this be worth it?' You do wonder if the batting, bowling and fielding can be this complicated. But then you also realise it's helping you stay in the game longer and possibly making you a better all-round cricketer.

I do feel like cutting loose sometimes but I understand that the pressure comes from the top and everyone has to satisfy someone else. The ACB have sponsors to keep happy so they pressure the coach, 'Let's get these guys super-fit'. The coach then works on us. They want us to be the best team ever and, in turn, we earn the most of any team in history. I also realise that a successful national team means that cricket as a sport will continue to prosper, as youngsters aspire to be like their heroes.

I am a bit from the old school, though, along with Ian Healy and Stephen. We're older than most of the others and come from a slightly earlier era. The new guys love the gym. It's how they've grown up. They were brought up on it and they want to train every day. We older ones have been caught a bit in the transition. Even when we're given a little time off, the younger players are looking for something to do. They have a completely different way of thinking. It's the era of the new professionalism. Geoff

Marsh might say, 'Okay, have a bit of time off', and they'll say 'No, let's go and have a hit in the nets'. I wouldn't dream of doing that. I think it starts at the Cricket Academy where the work ethic is very strong. Apart from Dennis Lillee and maybe the Chappells in Doug's era, the past players probably thought the gym routines were only for Olympic athletes.

You couldn't get away now with the things that the guys used to get up to in Doug's era. I'm not suggesting they were alcoholics but we almost can't even be seen in a bar now. The new approach is due to a mixture of pressures from sponsors, the ACB, the media and a busy fixture list.

Image is so important these days, both on and off the field. You do have to be aware that high profile sportsmen are fair game, not just for positive stories, but for negative stories and news as well.

CHAPTER FOURTEEN

THE FUTURE OF THE GAME

IF IT AIN'T BROKE,
DON'T FIX IT

'. . . I feel that one-day cricket will always be a game of chance, with both teams having an almost equal opportunity to win.'

Since Test cricket started in 1877, there have been very few rule changes. The first Australian team, which was an aboriginal side, included players such as Twopence and Dick a Dick. I have memorised their names from looking at photos at the SCG. How strange this game must have seemed to this first team, although their natural coordination and athleticism would have made them well-suited to play.

This initial team used balls which weighed the same as those used today, their bats were very similar, and they played by much the same rules. There have been a couple of changes to bring in leg-side fielding restrictions. Also, there are now limits on the number of short-pitched balls which can be bowled in any one over, and underarm bowling is now disallowed, but apart from these relatively minor changes, cricket is still the same game that it was more than 120 years ago.

I once said that there would have to be changes made to Test cricket to keep it viable when a general acceptance of one-day cricket had developed. I made this statement at a time when the Australian team had experienced a couple of seasons where they weren't really successful, and spectators had dropped off because the team was not winning. No doubt there will be similar cycles again in the future.

I feel that the other reason for the slump in crowd numbers was that there were no real stars in the team who could excite them with attacking play. However, Mark Taylor instigated a great turnaround in this, with his positive attacking form of leadership, and there has been a resurgence of interest. If this trend continues, with captains following the flair and individual stamp he put on the game, then I will need to retract my statement.

After watching the 1998–99 series with England in Australia, and seeing the crowds in attendance, one would have to say that there is nothing wrong with the rules at all. As has been shown in other sports, changing the rules is actually a very dangerous thing to do. There will always be spectators who don't like changes and once they are lost to the game, it is hard to win them back.

The experiment with the Super Sevens then Super Eights has hardly been a great success. The crowds don't appear to have accepted it, and we have to come back to thinking that there can't be too much wrong with the traditional rules and the game we have. It seemed in the Super series that nobody, including the players, knew exactly what was going on, and the matches were almost looked upon as a joke. 'Over the fence scores eight'—it just doesn't sound right. I can't imagine W.G. Grace giving his stamp of approval to such rules.

I personally feel that these kind of games are better left to teams playing social matches, where there are often many more than 12 in a team and something more than soft drinks during the breaks. It doesn't particularly matter if nobody understands the rules for these games.

One-day cricket attracts many different spectators (both male and female) including some who are happy to sit through a five-day Test match and still not see a result. People who enjoy one-day cricket more than Test cricket are usually those who want to see a result at the end of one day. They like the fact that they get to see both sides bat and bowl. There is nothing wrong with this preference, but I feel that one-day cricket will always be a game of chance, with both teams having an almost equal opportunity to win. The game originated for this purpose. On the other hand, if you want to find out which is the better cricket team, I feel you have to play a Test series.

The winner of the World Cup is not necessarily the best cricket team but more the luckiest in a short limited-over series. The most recent World Cup attracted huge crowds all over England, so I think this shows that there is a place for one-day cricket, and with more spectators coming through the turnstiles, the bank balances of the controlling boards are also healthier.

I do caution, however, that in Australia there is a risk of overkill with too many limited-over games. I feel that 15 games before the final series is far too many. It seems that spectators can lose their enthusiasm for these series before the two or three main games take place. The finals don't always attract full houses because the crowds no longer care who wins. This happened at the second final against England at the MCG in the 1998–99 series when only 25,000 people attended. I suppose the controlling bodies were happy to get that many, but for the ground which normally attracts the biggest cricket crowds in Australia, it's not such a good result.

Prior to the start of the 1998–99 English tour to Australia, there were suggestions that the series should be cut back to a three Test series. As it turned out, it was just as well this didn't happen, because the last two Test matches were excellent, with a great fightback by England. When England and Australia have strong sides there is strong interest in cricket. The English team has not been performing well for some time now, but during that 1998–99 tour of Australia, they showed definite signs of coming back to top form. The South African team bounced back very quickly after its exclusion from international competition and soundly defeated the West Indian team on its last tour of that country. If Pakistan can settle their political problems, the team will again be a force to be reckoned with, and India could use some more players to support the magnificent Tendulkar. However, while international sides are always going to vary in strength, I feel that enthusiasm for cricket will remain high while ever there are good contests between England and Australia.

The recent publicity, which is alleged to have involved player gambling, has not had a seriously detrimental affect on the game. I feel, however, that the players will need to exercise caution in the future because the spectators, who they rely on, will quickly turn off if there is any suggestion of match-fixing. The game's administrators will have to impose severe penalties for any future indiscretions.

International cricket has weathered two World Wars and is still going strong. It has also survived the Bodyline series and, more recently, World Series Cricket, but these obstacles did not seriously dent the appetite of the paying public and their love for the game. Today's children have many more sports to choose from both at school and outside school hours. When I was at school, we had football, tennis, athletics and cricket. This limited choice allowed us to have a go at all the sports on offer. There are now about three dozen sports to choose from, with a huge number of these offered in high school. It seems that many schools have now eliminated cricket from the choices on offer because of the time involved in matches, the sun-protection factor, and various other reasons. Our international team needs to contain outstanding players to capture the interest of these kids outside school hours and foster a strong junior competition. At this time, I feel that while there may not be as many children playing cricket the ones I come across at the many coaching camps I attend are very keen and have an extremely good knowledge of the game.

The structures we have in place now will need to be maintained to keep the Australian standard of cricket high. By this I mean that we need all the levels we currently have, from junior competition through to grade and then state level. We need to provide good umpires for all matches and encourage the holiday coaching camps. While the days of attracting big crowds to Sheffield Shield matches have probably gone, I feel that the administrators of the game will need to continue running these matches at a financial loss so that there is always a good base of up-and-coming players vying for a place in our international team.

The four-day Sheffield Shield matches provide the best nursery for future Australian players. I feel that this competition is the best in the world as far as helping players take the step from grade to international cricket. My old mate Rodney Marsh is also playing a big part in helping to secure a strong future for Australian cricket. Rod is in charge of the Cricket Academy, which is based in Adelaide. This institute is highly respected by all our young cricketers who attend it. The Academy takes in hand-picked, talented youths and has an excellent record in helping them graduate from there to Shield and Australian level. They are taken on tour to play against young interstate and international teams. When Rod once invited me to do some work at the Academy, I told him that his young charges wouldn't want to see me playing cross-batted shots. He just replied, 'I'm their coach. I want you to mix with them outside their coaching sessions as well.' At the Academy, the trainees are taught to behave off the field as well as on it. I don't know that I taught very well on that occasion because I haven't been invited back, but maybe it's Marshie's budget that needs to recover from my off-field lessons.

Rod seeks assistance from many ex-players as well as current players, and while he's in charge I know our next generation of Australian cricketers is in good hands. This is a wonderful innovation, which could be adopted by other countries around the world. I really don't envisage any major changes in cricket over the next couple of decades. As far as things stand at the moment, I think cricket management will do well to leave everything just as it is, and if tempted to make major changes, then apply the old saying, 'If it ain't broke, don't fix it'.

THE MONEY OR THE GAME?

*'Maybe some target should be in the grandstand
so we can score eights.'*

Cricket today is obviously leaning more towards one-day cricket than it is towards Test cricket. I don't think Test cricket will disappear, because the tradition is so strong, especially in England and Australia, but one-day cricket gives you a result on the day and I think that suits hectic lifestyles in the 1990s. It also suits our need for instant gratification.

It is completely understandable that most people have only one day to spend on spectator sport. Who has time to watch four or five days of cricket in a row? The 1999 season, for example, had more one-day games scheduled than ever before. The stadiums are filled for one-day matches so there is more money to be made. The cricket boards around the world can only survive if money is coming in, and there is no getting away from the fact that one-day cricket is the big source of revenue.

It is especially obvious that this is the way the game is going on the subcontinent. In India, Sri Lanka and Pakistan, there have been times when there's almost no one attending the Tests—perhaps 5,000 to 10,000 people at the most—although it must be acknowledged that the crowds were pretty strong in India in the 1998 season. In fact, there were huge crowds, particularly at the Calcutta Test, with over 50,000 spectators on a couple of days. That was great to see.

But the one-day games are always packed on the subcontinent. There's definitely going to be even more one-day cricket in the future. There are already tournaments everywhere, in places like Sharjah and Bangladesh, and even Canada. They'll have to be careful that players don't burn out. The players may just get sick of it and end up producing less than exciting cricket due to boredom, fatigue and injury. Cricket boards must find a happy medium to avoid these problems.

There's been a fair bit of speculation that eventually there'll be two different sides. The one-day and the Test side. Everyone is entitled to their opinions but I just can't see it happening. There'll always be players good enough or versatile enough to make both sides. Four or five players will always make both sides and they'll always pick their best 11 for both teams. It may even be that your best 11 Test players are also your best 11 one-day players. It just depends on the makeup of the teams at any given time.

Despite what I've already said, I believe that right now people who follow cricket think that Test cricket is the number one form of the game and will do for a while to come. If you ask people who their favourite players are, they're less likely to say Adam Dale, Chris Harris or Adam Hollioake, with all due respect to those guys. Most people will say the name of someone in the Test side. People in Australia and England still think of it as the 'real' game.

Our crowds, and those in England, are pretty comparable in size for one-dayers and Test matches. In England in 1997 we only played three one-day games, so people there are still putting Test cricket first. I think it is very important that England and Australia continue to show the rest of the cricketing countries that Test cricket should be their priority when drawing up itineraries. After all, we invented the game.

In the poorer countries, one-day cricket rules the game. Obviously there'd be a lot of reasons for that. I'd speculate that the reasons would include the fact that many fans wouldn't have televisions so they could only watch live games and perhaps only afford access on one day rather than over an extended time. Also, India isn't very successful at Test cricket and there are a lot of draws in their Test games. They win more often in one-day matches, and home crowds like to see their side win. The captain must lead the way here and play more positive Test cricket, as in our last series in India.

I do believe cricket is growing rather than being in decline. In each country the interest seems to be determined by how well the Test side is doing. In New Zealand at the moment, cricket isn't quite as big as rugby union because they aren't as successful. Here we have been successful, so cricket is currently very popular. Kids who are the future need role models and heroes, and at the moment, with the likes of McGrath, Healy, Warne and Stephen Waugh, we are blessed, and therefore interest is strong. There's no reason why Australia won't have a great side for many years to come because we have a very strong infrastructure.

It's the same for any sport or team. If you're not doing well, the fans drop off. The facilities we have here for players and junior cricketers are fantastic. We also have a lot of competitions, whereas in England, school cricket is almost non-existent, and it's the same in the West Indies.

In Australia we have the national titles at primary school,

high school, under-17s and under-19s levels, which all promote competitive cricket. We have the Cricket Academy in Adelaide, making sure promising players have the best in coaching and facilities to fine tune their game. Coaches headed by Rod Marsh, plus past and present greats like Ian and Greg Chappell, Dennis Lillee and Shane Warne are all available to pass on skills. Cricket in Australia does look healthy in the current climate, but we should never be complacent.

Part of the battle is to continue making the cricket interesting for the spectators. There's a new rule in England for one-day games, that I wholeheartedly approve of, aimed at making the game much more exciting to watch. If the bowler bowls a no-ball then the next ball is a free hit for the batsman. This immediately captures the attention of the spectators (not to mention the batsman) who are all eager to see the batsman cut loose and try to hit the ball out of the ground without fear of losing his wicket. I really like to see innovation like this, as long as it doesn't turn into a circus. I think these small changes don't necessarily interfere with the tradition and dignity of the game.

I don't actually think the game will change much in the next few decades. The basics will always be there. There may be some new equipment and we may be able to hit the ball further —more sixes. The bats are heavier than they used to be. We already hit the ball further and the cosmetics are more flamboyant, but it's still the same willow. One day they may invent a ball that's the same weight as the current balls but it won't hurt you.

I think the new rule of having fewer fieldsmen out of the circle in the Mercantile Mutual Cup is a good one and should alleviate some of the boredom in the middle part of those one-day games. Perhaps that will be introduced across the board. For mine I think it's a great rule and should be adopted.

I'd also like to see the removal of leg byes because the whole idea is to hit the ball. Why should you score for missing the very point of the game? I think that should happen in Tests and one-day games.

As I have said, I like the idea of adding more entertaining embellishments, like the one in which you win money for hitting the scoreboard. It doesn't radically change the game and doesn't tamper with the rules but it adds some entertainment value, which I think is important. I'd like to see incentives like that in international cricket too. Maybe some target should be in the grandstand so we can score eights. It would obviously have to be a very difficult shot. I know the traditionalists hate this sort of thing but you have to move with the times.

CHAPTER FIFTEEN

LAST WORD

NEVER TOO YOUNG TO MAKE
THE RIGHT CHOICE

*'I still feel I owe cricket a lot, and cricket
owes me nothing.'*

When people ask me questions about my life and career, I am
forced to reflect on the past years and then begin to wonder
whether or not I could have done better in my chosen sport.
Some people even try to compare sports, and query whether I
would choose cricket again. I think they are actually comparing
the financial rewards achieved from playing sport at an elite
level.

I can only speak from my own experience and of the chances
that came my way throughout my life. As a youngster I played
a lot of tennis and enjoyed quite a deal of success, winning competitions around Dungog. However, there is a huge difference
between competition in Dungog and the standard required to

play at Wimbledon. If, as a child, I had been able to look into a crystal ball and could see myself playing Davis Cup matches for Australia I might have given more consideration to pursuing a career in tennis.

It was yet another experience in the country, as we tried to watch the Davis Cup on a snowy, black-and-white television. We could hardly even make out the players, let alone the ball. It did, however, help to provide us with some of the atmosphere that we couldn't get listening to the radio.

We were in awe of the tennis players and golfers who were earning enormous sums of money even in those days. Like many other sports, those 'enormous sums' would be peanuts compared with what is earned by today's players. I am sure it will be the same comparing today's payments with those being paid in ten years' time, as the financial rewards continue to increase.

I did enjoy watching tennis as a kid, but I doubt I would have changed my mind about my chosen sport if I'd had that crystal ball. Apart from anything else, with cricket you have two chances. If you fail to be a good bat, you may make up for this failure by bowling well or taking amazing catches. When I was a kid, all my success was with the ball rather than the scoring of large numbers of runs. So it's funny how things can change.

Max Walker started his career as a batsman before he 'stumbled' into bowling. I reckon he developed his tangle-footed action as a ploy to confuse the umpires as well as the batsmen. With the old back-foot rule, the umpires wouldn't have known which was his back foot and which was his front. Max may have been equally confused.

John Gleeson was another cricketer who changed direction. He started his career as a wicket-keeper/batsman before adopting his unorthodox finger flicking bowling style. I feel that if players have a reasonable ability and can do something a little out of the ordinary, they will have success, particularly before the opposition can work out what they are doing and so develop strategies to combat these different styles. It took the opposition a long time to work out what Max and John were doing, so, like myself, their changes of direction were for the better.

My co-author had more choices in different sports that I did, however, I don't think Mark would have made an alternative career choice either. Mind you, I think we would both be very hard to please had we not been satisfied with our chosen lots. I have met numerous people, and I'm sure Mark has too, who would have given anything for the chance to play Test cricket for Australia. As stated earlier, we are two of the less than 400 over the past 120 years who have fulfilled our greatest ambitions to do just that, and we do appreciate our talents and fortunes. We have been so lucky but we also took our chances and accepted the challenges along the way.

There are so many others who, for various reasons, have not been so lucky. I have played with cricketers who I feel could have made it into the Australian team if they had been more dedicated to the task. I hope these fellows sleep okay and don't lie awake wondering how far they may have gone with a little more effort. Many such players didn't make it into first-class cricket, let alone the Australian team. But they made their choices at the time. The trouble is that time waits for no man. It passes all too quickly. My advice to young people who may feel they need to delay making the move to the city, or taking the chance to have a go at building a career in cricket is—do it now!

Improvements in roads, cars, trains and air travel have all made the city more accessible. I would say, don't let people talk you out of it with comments that you are still too young, or you need more experience. I hate to hear that someone is still too young, as time goes by so quickly.

In my opinion, young people should never be talked out of

having a go at something. They should instead be encouraged to take the chances as they come along. A person should never be considered too young. If they have a go and fail, they can try again the following year. Failure helps to strengthen the resolve to try harder, and if a person has enough willpower, he or she will find a way.

I coached Jim Maher, the Queensland batsman, when he was very young. I was in Cairns a number of years ago when a fellow came up to me and asked me to spend some time, when I returned to Sydney, finding a club in Sydney for young Jimmy. The fellow turned out to be Jim's father, Warren. The problem was that Jim was only seven at the time. Warren didn't have a lot of faith in the Queensland cricket selectors and when I returned some three or four years later he asked whether I had organised the Sydney club. He felt that Jimmy was now ready to make his move. I was not at all surprised to see Jim make it into the Queensland side. His father was prepared to let him leave home to improve his chances of playing sport at the top level, and I admire him for that.

The Australian cricket team should always be picked on the basis of the best available at the time of selection. During many tours, and in limited-overs matches, selections are sometimes based on the premise that a player may need a rest or that someone else needs to be given the chance. I wouldn't be at all happy if I was the player missing out on selection for either of these reasons. Wally Grout was one of Australia's great wicketkeepers and his saying was, 'Never give a sucker an even break'. I agree one hundred percent with Wally's philosophy. If someone should succeed when they are being 'tried' in your spot, it may be very hard to get back in.

Some of the suggestions currently being talked about for cricket give one food for thought, while others are just laughable.

I think one of the silliest I've heard recently is the suggestion of penalties for sledging opposition players. I feel that the umpires run the game on the field and they have done a good job controlling the players up until now, and this should not be changed. I can, however, accept the change in the no-ball rule currently under discussion here. This has, after all, already been changed twice since I first began playing. The first change was in fact that the extra run was added to the bowler's figures. It should be noted that these suggestions have not decreased the number of no-balls being bowled.

Some years ago, I suggested that the batsman should be given a free hit off the offending bowler's next delivery and I still feel this would force the bowler to watch his step more closely. With the front-foot rule, it is very difficult for a batsman to take full advantage of a no-ball because he doesn't have enough time after the umpire's call. If he was given a free hit off the next ball, excitement would be added to the match and the bowler might well be deterred from overstepping. I am pleased a trial has now been suggested for this change.

Since cricket is now a multimillion dollar business, it is good that the administration of cricket is also far more professional. In all walks of life, people seldom feel completely happy with their salaries. Cricketers are no exception to this, but I still feel that playing for one's country is such a honour and I know that I would happily play for Australia even if I wasn't paid (and I'm sure I wouldn't be alone).

Cricket still remains Australia's most popular sport. I don't mean any offence to the various football codes when I say this, but most of these are not considered truly national sports. Being part of cricket certainly helps me when I travel all over Australia on the speaking circuit. There are no real state boundaries. In my travels, I get to meet people from all different sports. I admire and respect many of them and try to take on board some of their wisdom. I have heard it said often that the second most important job in this country, after that of Prime Minister, is the job of the Australian cricket captain. I think this is true in many ways. I can't help but think of all the difficult decisions Steve Waugh has had to make in his new role, and I urge people not to be too critical.

I still feel I owe cricket a lot, and cricket owes me nothing. I may not have earned a fortune playing cricket over the years, but I have managed to make a living since my retirement because I played at the elite level. As I close, at the end of another book, I can only hope all future cricketers will feel the same respect I do. As I reflect on my life and career, I can happily say I feel satisfied.

A CAREER MADE TO ORDER

*'Teamwork takes you out of yourself and lifts
you to be a better person.'*

When I was at high school, a teacher by the name of Mr Perrot
was our careers adviser. He was a keen follower of all sports
including cricket, but when I said to him I wanted to be a
professional cricketer, he would say, 'Don't you think you
should have another career in mind to back you up in case that
doesn't eventuate?' As it happens, no other career ever took my
interest, so my mind was made up early and I stuck to it.

Looking back now I have no doubt that I have followed the
right path. I've watched my family and hundreds of others
going off on the train or in traffic jams to work in offices and
I realise how incredibly lucky I am. To do something you
absolutely love while representing your country, travelling
around the world and earning a comfortable living mostly

outdoors, takes a lot of beating and leaves very little or no room for complaint.

I have nothing whatsoever to complain about. There is little I have set out to achieve that hasn't happened. I can't think of many things I would do differently if I had the chance again. Captaincy is one area of the game in which I haven't had the experience, and before my career is over I would like to captain a first-class team. I might be a poor captain or I might be a good captain but it is one job that interests me.

I would also like a chance to play first-class cricket with my two younger brothers, Dean and Danny. They are definitely talented enough to succeed and it would be wonderful to see them get a chance and then to perform alongside them.

Obviously the 'Bookie Scandal' is one thing I would never get involved with again if I had my time over. You learn by your mistakes and I have certainly learned from mine.

One very minor regret is that, as a teenager, being such a keen sportsman, I probably pushed my growing body a little too hard. Soccer, cricket, indoor cricket, golf and tennis, involving playing or training virtually every day of the week, all took their toll. This was probably too much. As a result, stress fractures appeared in my back at the age of about 20. That certainly hindered me a bit. Next lifetime I'll take it a bit slower in my teens.

I honestly can't think of anything else I'd rather be doing but if I had to make a choice and cricket wasn't on the agenda, I'd perhaps want to be a professional tennis player or golfer. There's certainly less chance of injury in golf and the other thing that appeals to me is that there's no one to blame except yourself. You're completely in charge of your own destiny and there are fewer outside influences, whereas in cricket, the guy bowling to you can suddenly bowl a miracle ball and you can't do anything about it. Then there's the umpire. You can get good and bad decisions, but with golf it is completely in your hands, apart from the weather. I find that quite appealing.

What you miss out on in golf and tennis is the team spirit and that is the wonderful thing that I get from my career. Cricket teaches you to be unselfish. If you're playing and doing badly, but your team-mate does well, you can't be miserable and introspective. You have to rally and congratulate them. You have to share in their excitement. It teaches you to be thoughtful about other people and respect their wins and losses as much as your own. If someone gets a hundred and you get a duck you can't sit in the corner moping. Teamwork takes you out of yourself and lifts you to be a better person. That is something I will take away from my cricket career.

Next life I'll come back as a Greg Norman or a Rod Laver for a bit of variety, but if I come back as a cricketer again, that would be more than enough.

I can highly recommend this life to a teenager with designs on the baggy green cap. If you've got the talent and you're prepared to work at it then it is absolutely worth aiming for. I'm looking forward to a few more years ahead of me in this caper yet, and when it's all over, I know I'll still be connected to the game in some capacity. That's what I would hope for and want, in any case. Perhaps I should take Mr Perrot's advice and start thinking of some alternatives, but when you've had the best, it's hard to see what else there is.

CHAPTER SIXTEEN

OUR PLAYING RECORDS

WALTERS, KEVIN DOUGLAS

Born: 21 December, 1945, Dungog, NSW
Bats: Right-handed batsman
Bowls: Right-arm medium bowler

FIRST-CLASS CAREER
Debut: 1962–63 New South Wales v Queensland, Sydney

M	Inn	NO	Runs	50	100	Av
258	426	57	16,180	81	45	43.84

Ct	Balls	Mdns	Runs	Wkts	Av	5/Inn
149	13,251	304	6,782	190	35.69	6

Highest Score: 253 New South Wales v South Australia, Adelaide, 1964–65
Best Bowling: 7/63 New South Wales v South Australia, Adelaide, 1964–65

SHEFFIELD SHIELD CAREER
Debut: 1962–63 New South Wales v Queensland, Sydney

M	Inn	NO	Runs	50	100	Av
91	157	16	5,602	24	16	39.73

Ct	Balls	Mdns	Runs	Wkts	Av	5/Inn
49	7,688	190	3,609	110	32.81	4

Highest Score: 253 New South Wales v South Australia, Adelaide, 1964–65
Best Bowling: 7/63 New South Wales v South Australia, Adelaide, 1964–65

TEST CAREER
Debut: 1965–66 Australia v England, Brisbane

M	Inn	NO	Runs	50	100	Av
75	125	14	5,357	33	15	48.26

Ct	Balls	Mdns	Runs	Wkts	Av	5/Inn
43	3,295	79	1,425	49	29.08	1

Highest Score: 250 Australia v New Zealand, Christchurch, 1976–77
Best Bowling: 5/66 Australia v West Indies, Georgetown, 1972–73

FIRST CLASS FOR NEW SOUTH WALES
Debut: 1962–63 New South Wales v Queensland, Sydney

M	Inn	NO	Runs	50	100	Av
103	279	21	6,612	30	19	41.84

Ct	Balls	Mdns	Runs	Wkts	Ave	5/Inn
54	8,113	201	4,166	119	35.00	5

Highest Score: 253 New South Wales v South Australia, Adelaide, 1964–65
Best Bowling: 7/63 New South Wales v South Australia, Adelaide, 1964–65

INTERNATIONAL LIMITED-OVERS CAREER
Debut: 1970–71 Australia v England, Melbourne

M	Inn	NO	Runs	50	100	Av
28	24	6	13	2	–	28.50

Stk/Rt	Ct	Balls	Mdns	Runs	Wkts	Av	5/Inn
70.18	10	314	3	273	4	68.25	–

Highest Score: 59 Australia v Sri Lanka, The Oval, 1975
Best Bowling: 2/24 Australia v England, Birmingham, 1972

DOMESTIC LIMITED-OVERS CAREER
Debut: 1970–71 New South Wales v Queensland, Brisbane

M	Inn	NO	Runs	50	100	Av
13	11	3	340	4	–	42.50

Stk/Rt	Ct	Balls	Mdns	Runs	Wkts	Av	5/Inn
77.27	4	596	7	405	16	25.31	–

Highest Score: 71 New South Wales v Victoria, Melbourne, 1972–73
Best Bowling: 3/33 New South Wales v Victoria, Melbourne, 1980–81

WAUGH, MARK EDWARD

Born: 2 June, 1965, Canterbury, NSW
Bats: Right-handed batsman
Bowls: Right-arm off-spin bowler

FIRST-CLASS CAREER
Debut: 1985–86 New South Wales v Tasmania, Hobart

M	Inn	NO	Runs	50	100	Av
293	472	59	22,131	107	71	53.59

Ct	Balls	Mdns	Runs	Wkts	Av	5/Inn
331	14,308	489	7,655	194	39.46	3

Highest Score: 229* New South Wales v Western Australia, Perth, 1990–91
Best Bowling: 6/68 Australia XI v India Pres. XI, Patiala, 1996–97

SHEFFIELD SHIELD CAREER
Debut: 1985–86 New South Wales v Tasmania, Hobart

M	Inn	NO	Runs	50	100	Av
69	116	13	5,664	22	21	54.99

Ct	Balls	Mdns	Runs	Wkts	Av	5/Inn
83	3,559	119	1,849	51	36.25	–

Highest Score: 229* New South Wales v Western Australia, Perth, 1990–91
Best Bowling: 4/130 New South Wales v Queensland, Brisbane, 1985–86

TEST CAREER
Debut: 1990–91 Australia v England, Adelaide

M	Inn	NO	Runs	50	100	Av
90	151	10	6,042	35	16	42.85

Ct	Balls	Mdns	Runs	Wkts	Av	5/Inn
107	4,008	145	1,952	48	40.67	1

Highest Score: 153* Australia v India, Bangalore, 1997–98
Best Bowling: 5/40 Australia v England, Adelaide, 1994–95

FIRST CLASS FOR NEW SOUTH WALES
Debut: 1985–86 New South Wales v Tasmania, Hobart

M	Inn	NO	Runs	50	100	Av
84	140	19	6,848	31	23	56.60

Ct	Balls	Mdns	Runs	Wkts	Av	5/Inn
95	4,365	155	2,193	60	36.55	–

Highest Score: 229* New South Wales v Western Australia, Perth, 1990–91
Best Bowling: 4/130 New South Wales v Queensland, Brisbane, 1985–86

INTERNATIONAL LIMITED-OVERS CAREER
Debut: 1988–89 Australia v Pakistan, Adelaide

M	Inn	NO	Runs	50	100	Av
191	186	14	6,636	42	12	38.58

Stk/Rt	Ct	Balls	Mdns	Runs	Wkts	Av	5/Inn
76.94	76	3,351	10	2,658	81	32.81	1

Highest Score: 130 Australia v Sri Lanka, Perth, 1995–96
Best Bowling: 5/24 Australia v West Indies, Melbourne, 1992–93

DOMESTIC LIMITED-OVERS CAREER
Debut: 1985–86 New South Wales v Victoria, Sydney

M	Inn	NO	Runs	50	100	Av
35	34	3	1101	8	1	35.52

Stk/Rt	Ct	Balls	Mdns	Runs	Wkts	Av	5/Inn
80.72	19	729	7	569	18	31.61	–

Highest Score: 112 New South Wales v Victoria, North Sydney, 1991–92
Best Bowling: 3/23 New South Wales v Queensland, Brisbane, 1987–88

* not out

A PLACE IN HISTORY

AUSTRALIAN TEST CRICKET

Leading Run Scorers

Batsman	M	Inn	NO	Runs	HS	50	100	Av
AR Border	156	265	44	11,174	205	63	27	50.56
SR Waugh	115	185	35	7,622	200	41	19	50.81
MA Taylor	104	186	13	7,525	334*	40	19	43.50
DC Boon	107	190	20	7,422	200	32	21	43.66
GS Chappell	88	151	19	7,100	247*	31	24	53.86
DG Bradman	52	80	10	6,996	334	13	29	99.94
RN Harvey	79	137	10	6,149	205	24	21	48.42
ME Waugh	**90**	**151**	**10**	**6,042**	**153***	**35**	**16**	**42.85**
KD Walters	**75**	**125**	**14**	**5,357**	**250**	**33**	**15**	**48.26**
IM Chappell	76	136	10	5,345	196	26	14	42.42

NEW SOUTH WALES FIRST-CLASS CRICKET

Leading Run Scorers

Batsman	M	Inn	NO	Runs	HS	50	100	Av
AF Kippax	87	135	16	8,005	315*	18	32	67.27
MA Taylor	100	172	3	6,997	199	38	17	41.40
ME Waugh	**84**	**140**	**19**	**6,848**	**229***	**31**	**23**	**56.60**
J Dyson	94	170	17	6,773	241	37	14	44.27
KD Walters	**103**	**179**	**21**	**6,612**	**253**	**30**	**19**	**41.84**
W Bardsley	83	132	11	6,419	235	27	20	53.04
MG Bevan	74	129	27	6,308	203*	25	25	61.84
GRJ Matthews	135	200	35	6,226	184	32	9	37.98
RB McCosker	79	140	17	5,998	168	30	19	48.76
VT Trumper	73	123	9	5,823	292*	29	15	51.07

*not out